A friend of the gospel dare not mak~~e~~ this is precisely the sad state of affai~~rs~~ in the Western world today. Pastor S~~p~~... ~~...~~ ~~...~~ ~~book offers~~ needed clarity, especially for parents of prodigals. This book provides faithful pastoral guidance and serves as the best layman's guide to the law of God.

ROSARIA BUTTERFIELD
Author and speaker

The Psalmist could sing "Oh how I love your Law." Jesus declared that he had not come to abolish the law but to fulfill it. Paul reminded us that love fulfills the law. Yet sadly today, in many segments of the church, confusion reigns regarding the continued validity and use of the moral law of God. In this valuable little book, Stephen Spinnenweber begins to redress that confusion with some much needed clarity. The law is not the gospel, but the sweetness of the gospel can only be tasted when the law trains our palates on how bitter life is without it. The law cannot justify us, yet having been justified by grace through faith, the law shows us the way that sanctification always walks. This book will help you see that the law of God is the Christian's friend. It is the act of a friend to help us express the gratitude we feel for the Lord Jesus Christ (who bore the penalty of the law we have broken), by living a life of growing evangelical obedience—and this is exactly the role the law plays in the life of a Christian. This book will help you make progress in a life of cheerful, grateful, law keeping, and for that we are deeply thankful.

DAVID STRAIN
Senior Minister, First Presbyterian Church
Jackson, Mississippi

Can you say with the apostle Paul, "I delight in the law of God according to the inward man"? That ought to be the heart-testimony of every redeemed sinner. If you are not sure how or why a Christian could, or should, or would speak in that way, then Stephen Spinnenweber's short treatment on loving the law might help. You need not agree with all his conclusions and suggestions to appreciate the underlying simplicity and sweetness of his thoughts on the law of God, for when the Spirit of the living God writes the law of God on our hearts, then we say with the godly through the ages, "Your law is my delight!"

Jeremy Walker
Pastor, Maidenbower Baptist Church
Crawley, England

In *Loving the Law*, Stephen Spinnenweber leaves no stone unturned in revealing the importance and nuances of the Law of God to the reader. This is a subject that every Christian should desire to master for the good of their soul and walk with Christ; and here is a book that provides a readable, engaging, and applicable primer for that very purpose. Spinnenweber's work is thoroughly biblical and ably conveys the traditional Reformed teaching regarding the Law. The writing rings with conviction along with true pastoral care. If you read this book, prepare to be challenged, edified, and encouraged.

Jason Helopoulos
Senior Pastor, University Reformed Church
East Lansing, Michigan

LOVING THE LAW

The Law of God in the
Life of the Believer

STEPHEN
SPINNENWEBER

CHRISTIAN
FOCUS

Copyright © Stephen Spinnenweber 2025

paperback ISBN 978-1-5271-1252-0
ebook ISBN 978-1-5271-1311-4

10 9 8 7 6 5 4 3 2 1

Published in 2025

by

Christian Focus Publications Ltd.,

Geanies House, Fearn, Ross-shire

IV20 1TW, Great Britain.

www.christianfocus.com

Cover design by Rubner Durais

Printed and bound by
Bell and Bain Glasgow

Contents

Foreword

Christians struggle with the law of God in at least two ways. First, they struggle in *interpreting* God's Law. So much of the Bible contains commands from God. There are entire Old Testament books devoted to laws regarding sacrifices, purity, and the proper role of civil authorities in Israel. How are these to be understood? Should they essentially be ignored by Christians today? What role do they play in our lives?

There is also the question of commands in general. Are God's commands (whether in the Old Testament or the New) simply intended to show us our inability to keep any command fully? Are Christians expected to keep them at all?

This question of *interpretation* has been answered in many different ways throughout the history of the church. Some earnest Bible-believing Christians have concluded that the only laws that matter are those in the New Testament, or, perhaps in more extreme cases, only those found in the epistles of the New Testament. Still others have understood that all the laws need to receive some attention, but only insofar as studying the law points us to the grace of God—the only remedy for our persistent law-breaking.

But *interpreting* the law of God is only one of the major questions that emerges from a careful study of the law-portions of Scripture. Another important issue is the *observance* or *application* of the law. How should the law be observed today?

If we grant that Christians must study the law, then how should they apply it? Is a theocratic government (similar to Old Testament Israel before the exile) required? If not, on what grounds can we assert this? How strictly should we apply God's Law today? Aside from practical questions, does legal observance lead to legalism and a denial of the grace of the gospel?

Because of these thorny questions, many are content to ignore the law or to view it in a negative light. Sometimes, the words of the Apostle Paul are cited to bolster this perspective. After all, Paul writes, "For by works of the law no human being will be justified in his sight, since through the law comes knowledge of sin" (Rom. 3:20); and "For the letter kills, but the Spirit gives life" (2 Cor. 3:6b), or, again, "For all who rely on works of the law are under a curse; for it is written, 'Cursed be everyone who does not abide by all things written in the Book of the Law, and do them'" (Gal. 3:10).

But what about the ways that other passages of Scripture speak of the law? Jesus says, "For truly, I say to you, until heaven and earth pass away, not an iota, not a dot, will pass from the Law until all is accomplished" (Matt. 5:18). It seems, in many cases, as if keeping and loving the law is the key to the blessed life. To give just one example, consider these words from Psalm 119:

> Blessed are those whose way is blameless,
>   who walk in the law of the Lord!
> Blessed are those who keep his testimonies,
>   who seek him with their whole heart,
> who also do no wrong,
>   but walk in his ways!
> You have commanded your precepts

to be kept diligently.
Oh that my ways may be steadfast
    in keeping your statutes!
Then I shall not be put to shame,
    having my eyes fixed on all your commandments.
I will praise you with an upright heart,
    when I learn your righteous rules.
I will keep your statutes;
    do not utterly forsake me! (vv.1-8).

In the end, our questions will not be answered by pitting one set of texts against another; still less by ignoring whichever perspective on the law seems unattainable or unsuited to our understanding of the Christian life. We cannot ignore any portion of God's Word—including His Law.

This book goes a long way to explaining a proper, fully-orbed view of the law. It is not overly technical, but neither does it avoid difficult issues or complex questions. It is the kind of book that Christians—especially those who struggle with questions about the law of God—should read and digest carefully.

Jonathan L. Master
President
Greenville Presbyterian Theological Seminary

Acknowledgments

Of the many people that I need to thank for making this book a reality, my wife and best friend, Sarah's name belongs at the top of the list. Your love, support, and encouragement to me every step of the way was a visible reminder of Proverbs 18:22, "He who finds a wife finds a good thing and obtains favor from the Lord." None of this would have been possible without you.

Thank you, Colin Fast, for being an excellent editor and even better friend. Your attention to detail and commitment to clarity greatly improved the manuscript and your zeal for the Reformed faith is truly an inspiration to me. I consider it a privilege to be a co-laborer for Christ with you.

I'd also like to thank my father-in-law, Tim Broadwick, for acting as an extra set of editorial eyes and for his attentive ears as I verbally processed my way through the book. I couldn't ask for a better father-in-law. Thank you.

And thank you too to the small army of conversation partners who offered feedback on my manuscript and/or ushered me on toward the finish line. Thanks especially to Dr. Jonathan Master, Dr. Scott Cook, Jonathan Cruse, Zackary Groff, Sean Morris, Derrick Brite, Matt Adams, and Nick Bullock.

Introduction

"How do you use the law of God?"

Before discovering the riches of the Reformed faith, I would not have known how to answer that question. Frankly, I wouldn't have understood the question at all; instead, I would find myself asking: "By 'law' do you mean the sacrifices of the Old Testament or the Ten Commandments? And what do you mean by 'use'? Since the law was given through Moses and grace and truth came through Jesus Christ (John 1:17), why would we use the law if it only condemns? Leave the law in the Old Testament where it belongs." I suspect that most professing Christians today, if asked the same question, would respond with the same confusion.

As I would later come to discover, such an attitude toward the law likens it to a primitive relic kept behind museum glass, left to gather dust with the passage of time. What John Newton said of the church in his day could easily be said of the church in our own: "Ignorance of the nature and design of the law is at the bottom of most religious mistakes."[1] Think of it—what is self-righteousness but a woefully low view of what the law

---

1 John Newton, *The Works of John Newton* (Edinburgh, UK: Banner of Truth Trust, 2015), 240.

really requires? What is a lack of assurance of salvation but forgetting that our acceptance with God is not based on our obedience to the law? What is backsliding and loose living but a failure to see that the law is not contrary to our joy but the means whereby we experience true joy (Ps. 119:35, 47, 143)? So many of our problems are traceable to ignorance of the law's meaning and purpose.

Reformed theology offers a positive (and threefold!) answer to this important question. John Calvin, in his *Institutes of the Christian Religion,* introduces the reader to what the Reformed tradition calls "the three uses of the law."[2] By "law" Calvin was speaking narrowly of the Moral Law, which is most clearly summarized in the Ten Commandments.[3] Of course, this does not mean that Calvin, or the Reformed tradition as a whole, believes there is no benefit in studying broader Old Testament laws.[4] They are anything but useless. They hold tremendous instructive value even today; they were written for our instruction (1 Cor. 10:11). Nevertheless, the Moral Law stands alone in its continuance as a perpetual rule of life for believers even after Christ's death and resurrection. The question is—why? Are Christians being selectively ethical, choosing to follow only the laws that they like and casting

2 John Calvin, *Institutes of the Christian Religion,* transl. Henry Beveridge (Peabody, MA: Hendrickson Publishers, 2008), 2.7.6-17

3 Or, as the Westminster Shorter Catechism (WSC) puts it, the Moral Law is "summarily comprehended in the Ten Commandments" (see Questions 40 and 41). From this this point forward, the terms "Ten Commandments," "Moral Law," and "law" will be used interchangeably.

4 The Reformed tradition has historically distinguished between the Moral, Civil, and Ceremonial Laws of the Old Testament. The Moral Law is found in the Ten Commandments; the Civil and Ceremonial Laws are found throughout the rest of the Old Testament and are specific and situational applications of the Moral Law. This threefold division of the law will be clarified in chapter one. For a modern defense of this idea, see: Philip S. Ross, *From the Finger of God: The Biblical and Theological Basis for the Threefold Division of the Law* (Fearn: Christian Focus, 2011).

aside all the ones they don't? This is a common objection to the Christian faith and one for which believers should have a ready answer (1 Pet. 3:15). Chapter one will tackle this issue head-on by defining the three basic *types* of law, and exaplain why the Moral Law remains binding upon all men and the Ceremonial and Civil Laws do not.

Chapter two will unpack each of the Ten Commandments, using the Westminster Shorter and Larger Catechisms' expositions of the commandments as a guide.[5] Before we can even speak about *how* to use the Moral Law, we first need to know what it is and the breadth and depth of what it requires. This is the point at which Jesus corrected the shallow interpretation of the scribes and Pharisees. They mistakenly assumed that they knew God's law exhaustively and so obeyed it perfectly. Together with the rich young man they thought, "All these I have kept" (Matt. 19:20). But when Jesus examined the Moral Law and exposed their pride and hypocrisy, then and only then could the law begin to do its good work of bringing Christ's hearers to a knowledge of their sin and their need of His perfect righteousness. We need to interpret the Ten Commandments the way that Jesus did. Many professing believers are indeed familiar with the *letter* of the Ten Commandments—they can recite a handful of commandments from memory—but far fewer have truly grasped and meditated upon the *spiritual* nature of the law. This chapter will aim to take the reader deeper, to show that there is more to the law than at first meets the eye.

The remaining three chapters will examine each of the three uses of the Moral Law and how it functions like a mirror, muzzle, and map.[6] When used properly, the law brings

---

5 The reader will want to keep Larger Catechism Q. 99, with its eight rules for rightly interpreting the Ten Commandments, close at hand as they work their way through this chapter.

6 These three images are not unique to me. See Phil Ryken's book, *Written in Stone* (Phillipsburg, NJ: P&R Publishing, 2010), 27, where he acknowledges

conviction, protection, and direction. We *need* the law to reveal our sin, to restrain sin in us and in our neighbors lest society completely unravel, and to help us answer the age old question, "How do I live a life that is pleasing to the Lord?" For a generation that struggles with aimlessness and lacks a sense of purpose, the law acts as man's true north, pointing us straight to the will of God for our lives. You will notice in these chapters that I am deeply indebted to men like John Calvin, Anthony Burgess, Samuel Bolton, Stephen Tyng, and, of a more recent vintage, Ernest Kevan. Their wisdom and insights have inspired a deeper love and appreciation of the law of God within me. This book would not be in your hands were it not for these men. As I pass along just a handful of the many gems I have mined from their writings, my prayer is that their words will have the same profound effect upon you as they have had on me.

My ultimate aim in this book is to convince you that the believer's growth in grace will not be inhibited but enhanced by a careful study of the Moral Law. Many, for fear of appearing legalistic, have avoided studying the law altogether. Others, when they do encounter the imperatives of Scripture, will rush to say, "But of course none of us have or can obey this command perfectly. But don't worry, Jesus did. He kept the law for you." Soundbites like this, though true as far as they go, effectively drain any sense of moral oughtness from the command in question. The hearer is left floating in an ethical no-man's land, wondering, "So what *am* I supposed to do now?" The good news of what Christ has done does not negate our responsibility to do what God commands. Imperatives do indeed drive us back to the indicative of Christ's person and

---

that he heard these three images from another preacher (who I expect heard them from another preacher before him, who heard them from a preacher before him ...).

work, and yet they are no less imperatival. God commands His redeemed people to strive for holiness (Heb. 12:14). Many of us have been conditioned to think that the law itself is bad. This book will argue just the opposite—the law of God is good and is the key to a truly blessed life when used in the way that God purposes—not as a means of earning eternal life, but of bringing us to Christ for our justification and conforming us into His glorious image through the power of the Spirit in our sanctification (Rom. 8:29). We should not wince, but rejoice over God's law.

Instead of seeing the Ten Commandments like an antiquated museum piece, I hope that you will view them more like a cherished cast-iron skillet that has been passed down through the family—something that was made long ago, but, if handled properly, will prove to be more and more useful as time goes on. May the Lord through this study cause us all to say together with David, "Oh how I love your law! It is my meditation all the day" (Ps. 119:97).

1

What Is the Law?

"Okay, so let me get this straight. You're saying that the Bible teaches that sex outside of monogamous, heterosexual marriage is a sin. Doesn't the Bible also say you shouldn't eat shellfish and pork? Do you mean to tell me you've never eaten a hotdog, bacon, or a (Maryland) crab cake? And what about that shirt you're wearing? Unless that's 100 percent cotton, the Bible says you're in sin because Leviticus 19:19 says you're not supposed to wear clothes made of two kinds of material. Does that *not* strike you as hypocritical? And what about all the places in the Old Testament where people were stoned for their 'sin'? Why don't Christians stone people now if they think they're so sinful? Do you think I should be stoned?"

If you haven't been on the business end of a machine-gun interrogation like this before, chances are you know someone who has. If believers go into such a conversation without a firm grasp of the meaning and application of the law of God, questions like these will be particularly jarring to their faith. They may think, "Maybe they have a point. Why do I follow some of God's commands but not all of them? Could it be that

I have been too closed-minded on this issue? Why have I never thought about this before?" The time to start thinking through the law of God is now, not in the middle of a barrage of "what-about" questions. To that end, this chapter will define the three types of law in Scripture and explain why one type continues to serve as a permanent rule of obedience for all men and the other two do not.

Three Types of Law

The word "law" is used in a wide variety of ways in Scripture. The Hebrew word *torah,* which means "teaching" and is typically translated "law," occurs hundreds of times in the Old Testament. Sometimes it refers to the entirety of God's special revelation (Ps. 1:2, 19:7), other times it refers to the Old Testament as a period of time (Matt. 5:17; Luke 16:16), and at other times more narrowly to the five books of Moses (Gen.–Deut., cf. Luke 24:44; John 1:45, 12:34; 1 Cor. 9:9). In two noteworthy places in the prophets, *torah* even refers to the good news of the gospel going forth from Jerusalem and extending its saving influence to all nations:

> "Come, let us go up to the mountain of the Lord,
> to the house of the God of Jacob,
> that he may teach us his ways
> and that we may walk in his paths."
> For out of Zion shall go forth the law,
> and the word of the Lord from Jerusalem
> (Isa. 2:3, cf. Micah 4:2).

Of all the New Testament writers, the Apostle Paul uses the term "law" (*nomos*) and its derivatives (lawful, lawfully, etc.) more than any other writer. In fact, Paul's usages in the books of Romans and Galatians alone account for almost half of all usages in the New Testament. The biggest challenge of interpreting Paul is trying to understand what *kind* of law he is talking about in any given context. For example, in Romans 3:20, Paul uses "law" to refer to the Ceremonial, Civil, and Moral Laws collectively in order to stress that man can in no way be justified by his own obedience.[1] In Romans 7:25, "law" refers to the sinful, fleshly principle against which Paul wrestles and contends in his inner man. It's shorthand for remaining sin. Then in Romans 8:2, Paul speaks of a "law of the Spirit of life" and a "law of sin and death," which refer to the rules or standards by which one lives their life, only to shift gears in verse 3 to say that God, through the sending of His Son, accomplished what the *Moral Law* could not do due to our sinful flesh—it could not serve as the basis of our right standing before God.

Admittedly, trying to keep the many uses of "law" straight in one's mind can be a dizzying task, even to the most careful reader of Scripture. The Scottish preacher John Colquhoun, however, helps us to cut through some of this confusion. Colquhoun referred to these various usages of law (references to Scripture itself, the Old Testament as an era, a spiritual principle, etc.) as the "unrestricted sense" of law—when the term is being used to speak of something other than a divine precept or command. The "restricted or limited sense" of law, he writes:

> is employed to express the rule which God has prescribed to His rational creatures in order to direct and oblige them to the right performance of all their duties to Him. Or in other words, it is used to signify the declared will of God, directing and obliging mankind to do that which pleases Him, and to abstain from what displeases Him.[2]

---

1 William Hendriksen, *Exposition of Paul's Epistle to the Romans*, vol. 2. New Testament Commentary (Grand Rapids, Mich: Baker Book House, 1980), 124.

2 John Colquhoun, *The Law and the Gospel* (Grand Rapids, MI: Reformation Heritage Books, 2023), 9.

The Ceremonial, Civil, and Moral Laws all fall under this restricted sense of law. In each, the Lord commands His people to do certain things and forbids them to do others. The content of the commands and rationales behind them differ, but they are alike in that they communicate the duties God requires of man.

The Ceremonial Law
Made to Be a Shadow

The Ceremonial Law regulated the worship of God's people in the Old Testament period. These laws governed everything from the consecration of priests (Lev. 8), the fashioning of tabernacle and temple furnishings (Exod. 25–30), and the necessary steps for offering right sacrifices (Lev. 1–7). The rites and ceremonies of the Ceremonial Law were all typological, meaning they foreshadowed the ministry of Christ and had no power in and of themselves to save the one who made the offering. Hebrews 10:1-4 makes this very point:

> For since the law has but a shadow of the good things to come instead of the true form of these realities, it can never, by the same sacrifices that are continually offered every year, make perfect those who draw near. Otherwise, would they not have ceased to be offered, since the worshipers, having once been cleansed, would no longer have any consciousness of sins? But in these sacrifices there is a reminder of sins every year. For it is impossible for the blood of bulls and goats to take away sins.

The writer of Hebrews argues that the sacrifices of the Old Testament were made to be provisional, not permanent; they were shadows, not the source or substance of salvation. Had the blood of bulls and goats been the permanent solution to Israel's sin problem, why then did they need to be offered every year? Once should have been enough. Moreover, if the sacrifices and ceremonies *were* able "to make perfect those who drew near" then why did Christ come in the incarnation at all? His sacrifice would have been superfluous, as Paul writes, "... for if righteousness were through the law, then Christ died for no purpose" (Gal. 2:21). The bloody sacrifices of the Ceremonial Law were designed to open the eyes of the one who offered it to the severity of their sin, and point forward to the "offering of the body of Jesus Christ *once* for all" (Heb. 10:10). Only Jesus could truly say, "It is finished" (John 19:30) when He gave up His spirit and breathed His last. Jesus paid it all.

John the Baptist's ministry demonstrates that Old Covenant believers were meant to see the Ceremonial Law in typological and shadowy terms. When John saw Jesus, the shadow-caster, approaching him near the Jordan river, he said of Him, "Behold, the Lamb of God, who takes away the sin of the world" (John 1:29). John understood that the many lambs that were slain day after day in the temple served as mere glimpses of this lamb, the lamb who would be stricken, smitten, and afflicted, carrying the griefs and sorrows of His people upon His shoulders (Isa. 53:4).

Jesus Himself instituted the Lord's Supper on the night of the Passover. In so doing, He was communicating to His disciples that He was the new Passover Lamb and that His blood would cause the wrath of the Father to pass over His chosen people (Exod. 1; Lev. 23:4-8; Matt. 26:26-29). The types and shadows of the Ceremonial Law find their fulfillment in the life, death, and resurrection of Jesus Christ (Matt. 5:17-18). The rites and ceremonies were not the end, they were a means to the end of glorifying Jesus Christ.

The Abrogation of the Ceremonial Law

Because Christ satisfied the demands of the Ceremonial Law on behalf of His people, Scripture teaches that believers are no longer required to keep the Ceremonial Law. In Hebrews 10:5-7, we read that Christ's incarnation, death, and resurrection pleased the Father in a way that the sacrifices and offerings of the Old Testament never did or could. The writer quotes Psalm 40:6-7 where David says, "Sacrifices and offerings you have not desired, but a body you have prepared for me; in burnt offerings you have taken no pleasure. Then I said, 'Behold, I have come to do your will, O God, as it is written of me in the scroll of the book.'" In verses 8-10, the writer of Hebrews interprets David's words messianically, making Christ the speaker. Christ came to do His Father's will by taking a human body prepared for Him and offering Himself as the once-for-all, atoning sacrifice for His people's sin. In so doing, verse 9 says, "He does away with the first order to establish the second." Hebrews 8:13 says the same, "In speaking of a new covenant, he makes the first one obsolete." Christ's death and resurrection did away with the first order, the sacrifices "offered according to the law." Having served their purpose, the ceremonies of the Old Testament are set aside to make way for the second order, the New Covenant under which God's people now live.

This doing away with (that is, the abrogation of) the first order is pictured, quite dramatically, in the tearing of the temple veil in two after Christ's crucifixion. That the curtain was torn from top to bottom signified God's making a new way for His people to commune with Him apart from the offering of animal sacrifices and the mediation of an earthly high priest (the central figure of the Ceremonial Law). Through Christ, the eternal high priest after the order of Melchizedek (Ps. 100:4; Heb. 7), "we have confidence to enter the holy places by the blood of Jesus, by the new and living way that he opened for us through the curtain, that is, through his flesh..." (Heb. 10:19-20). In and through Christ, all of God's people are "a chosen race, a royal priesthood, a holy nation, a people for his own possession..." (1 Pet. 2:9). Through Christ our Great High Priest, believers enjoy privileges that Old Covenant saints only dreamed of—we are all priests with bold access to God, and seated with the risen and reigning Christ in the heavenly places (Eph. 2:6).

The Antitype > The Type

Theologians will often speak of Old Testament types (the Greek word *tupos* means "figure, model, or example") that foreshadowed the person and work of Christ who is their ultimate reference point (anti-type). The Ceremonial Law was a blessing in so far as it trained the expectations of the Israelites to seek the One that was to come. And so, when Christ came in the fullness of time, it came time to retire the Ceremonial Law lest Christ's people should look to the blood of bulls and goats for their salvation instead of Christ Himself. That is the thrust of the entire book of Hebrews—"Do not turn back to the Ceremonial Law as though it had the power to save you. It never did. If you turn to the Ceremonial Law for your justification, you are turning away from Christ the Justifier. Christ is better. There is no salvation apart from or beside Him. Press on in Him."

I like to illustrate the relationship between the Ceremonial Law and Christ by likening it to the relationship between a movie trailer and the movie itself. A movie trailer is an effective tool for introducing viewers to key elements of a movie's plot and whetting their appetites for its release. Once the movie premieres, however, the trailer becomes obsolete. How strange would it be if, after a film was released, a viewer chose to keep watching the movie trailer instead of the movie itself? The trailer, by its very nature, was provisional—it was never meant to hold the viewer's attention indefinitely but direct their attention to something greater than itself. So it is with the Ceremonial Law. Christ has come, and so in obedience to the command of the Father from atop the Mount of Transfiguration, God's people are to listen and look to Jesus Christ alone, the one of whom the Law and the prophets both spoke (Luke 9:35).[3]

The Civil Law

The Civil and Ceremonial Laws are inextricably linked. By virtue of the fact that both were instituted by God through Moses (Civil Law in Exod. 21–23, Ceremonial Law in Exod. 25–30), they are often referred to together as the Mosaic Law.[4] Most Christians readily understand why the Ceremonial Law passed away with the coming of Christ, but comparatively few have as robust an understanding of why the Civil Law has passed away as well. This section will highlight reasons for the passing away of the Civil Law that apply equally to the Ceremonial Law (e.g. their function as types), and anticipate common objections to the Civil Law's passing away.

The German Reformed theologian, Zacharias Ursinus, defines the Civil (Judicial) Law this way:

The judicial laws were those which had respect to the civil order or government, and the maintenance of external propriety among the Jewish people according to both tables

---

3 Notice that Moses and Elijah also appeared atop the Mount of Transfiguration with Christ. This teaches us that Christ was the one to whom the Law (Moses) and the prophets (Elijah) pointed. In listening to Christ, we are, in effect listening to Moses and the prophets. Christ came in fulfillment of all that they prophesied.

4 This designation does not deny that the Ten Commandments were in force during the Mosaic era. Though God did reveal the Moral Law to Israel in Exodus 20, it was binding on all men long before the Ceremonial and Civil Laws that were established at Sinai for the first time. The Moral Law was not *uniquely* Mosaic (Rom 2:15) or revealed to Israel *particularly* like the Ceremonial and Civil Laws, hence the terminological distinction.

of the Decalogue; or it may be said that they had respect to the order and duties of magistrates, the courts of justice, contracts, punishments, fixing the limits of kingdoms. These laws God delivered through Moses for the establishment and preservation of the Jewish commonwealth, binding all the posterity of Abraham, and distinguishing them from the rest of mankind until the coming of the Messiah; and that they might also serve as a bond for the preservation and government of the Mosaic polity, until the manifestation of the Son of God in the flesh...[5]

Notice two important elements of Ursinus's definition. First, the Civil Law was given particularly to Israel as a theocratic nation. It was not laid down as a universal rule by which every nation was and is expected to adhere in every detail. Ursinus stresses that it was for the "Jewish people" that the Civil Law was given, for "the establishment and preservation of the *Jewish commonwealth.*" The stipulations and penalties of the Civil Law served "as a bond for the preservation and government of the *Mosaic polity.*" Therefore, when the Mosaic polity passed away, we are meant to infer that the specific applications of the Civil Law passed away with it. This is the second noteworthy element in Ursinus's definition—that like the Ceremonial Law to which it was tied, the Civil Law was a temporary, positive law of God that distinguished Israel "from the rest of mankind *until the coming of the Messiah.*"[6]

Ursinus's definition, however, prompts the question, "If the Civil Law of Israel was for 'the maintenance of external propriety among the Jewish people *according to both tables of the Decalogue*' (i.e. the Ten Commandments/Moral Law) then

---

5 Zacharius Ursinus, *Commentary on the Heidelberg Catechism*. trans. G.W. Williard (Grand Rapids, MI: Netherlands Reformed Book & Publishing, 2015), 491.

6 A discussion on what is meant by positive law will come later in this chapter.

why don't we believe that the Civil Law continues to be binding like the Moral Law is?"

This is a fair question. To be sure, the Civil Law touched on issues that fell within the scope of the Moral Law. The Civil Law included penalties for sexual immorality, theft, murder, and bearing false-witness.[7] This does not mean, however, that the specific judicial enforcements of the Moral Law within Israel remain in force as long as the Moral Law does. The Westminster Divines write, "To them [Israel] also, as a body politic, He gave sundry judicial laws, which expired together with the State of that people; not obliging any other now, further than the general equity thereof may require" (WCF 19:4).

The Westminster Divines, like Ursinus before them, believed that the Civil Law expired "together with the State of that people." When Solomon's temple was destroyed and the Jews were carried into exile by the Babylonians in 586 B.C., Israel ceased to be a theocratic nation (State) as they had been up to that point in time. Even after their restoration to the land and rebuilding of the temple, the absence of the *shekinah* glory filling the second temple as it had the first, coupled with the woeful spiritual condition of the scribes, Pharisees, and Sadducees in Jesus' day indicates that Israel was still in *spiritual* exile. The returned exiles were a shell of their former selves; Israel was Israel in name only. Add on top of this Israel's inability to exercise the civil laws of the Old Testament while under Roman rule (John 18:31), the crucifixion of Jesus who was great David's greater son and the rightful King of the Jews, and the destruction of the second temple in A.D. 70, and it becomes abundantly clear that Israel ceased to be the "body politic" that God had established at Mount Sinai.

---

7 Several Puritan writers taught that the Ceremonial Law was an appendix to the first four commandments of the Decalogue and the Civil Law was an appendix to the latter six commandments.

What Does "General Equity" Mean?

But what did the Divines mean when they spoke about the "general equity" of the Civil Law? For starters, we should note that "general" is the opposite of "specific." The specific judicial laws of Israel are "not obliging any other now." Any attempt to reinstate the Civil Law of Israel in its *exact* form today would be to reverse the trajectory of redemptive history. As Chad Van Dixhoorn writes, "There is much to learn from these ceremonial and judicial laws. But to continue the judicial laws and their penalties would be to forget that the new Israel is the church, and not some political nation on earth."[8] The goal of Old Testament Israel was the spiritual Israel of God (Gal. 6:16). The goal of the type is always the antitype, never the reverse, as we are told in the book of Hebrews. General equity then refers to the general principles of divine justice and equity among men to which the Civil Law pointed.

The Westminster Divines cited 1 Corinthians 9:8-10 to illustrate what they meant by general equity. In 1 Corinthians 9 Paul defends his right, as an Apostle, to have his material needs met by those who spiritually benefited from his labors (v. 11). To ground his argument, Paul, beginning in verse 8, points back to the Civil Law (Deut. 25:4) where the particular commandment refers not to ministerial compensation but to livestock!

> Do I say these things on human authority? Does not the Law say the same? For it is written in the Law of Moses, "You shall not muzzle an ox when it treads out the grain." Is it for oxen that God is concerned? Does he not certainly speak for our sake? It was written for our sake, because the plowman should plow in hope and the thresher thresh in hope of sharing in the crop. If we have sown spiritual things among you, is it too

---

8   Chad B. Van Dixhoorn, *Confessing the Faith: A Reader's Guide to the Westminster Confession of Faith* (Edinburgh, Scotland: The Banner of Truth Trust, 2016), 247.

much if we reap material things from you? If others share this
rightful claim on you, do not we even more? (1 Cor. 9:8-12)

According to Paul, the general equity (the heart) of this
commandment is the ethical principle, "pay the worker what
he is due." Or, as Luke 10:7 puts it, "the laborer deserves his
wages." It is this general principle of justice ("You shall not
steal") and not necessarily the specific application of that
principle to oxen that remains binding upon all men.

The Civil Law as a Tutor

Even if they've never stopped to consider it, every parent knows
intuitively that the manner of enforcing a moral principle can
change without changing the principle itself. Take the fifth
commandment as an example—honor your father and your
mother. The rules and consequences that a parent lays down
for a three-year-old will look very different from those laid
down for a sixteen-year-old. For the three-year-old, the rules
will be "Don't hit your sibling. Pick up your toys. Don't talk to
strangers." The consequences for disobedience will be losing
screen time, sitting in timeout, or an early bedtime. For the
sixteen-year-old the rules will be "Don't text and drive. No
video games until your homework is complete. Be back no
later than ten o'clock." The consequences for disobedience may
be losing video game privileges, taking away their cell phone,
or not being allowed to borrow the family car. Is one set of
rules or consequences more faithful to the fifth commandment
than the other? No, they are equally faithful. The general equity
of the fifth commandment—honoring father and mother—
remains the same, though the mode of expressing and enforcing
the principle changes according to the age of the child. For the
same reason we would think it strange if a parent put their
sixteen-year-old child in "timeout" as though he were three,
neither should the church strive to live under the same rules to

which it was subject during its infancy in the Old Testament. With the ministry of Jesus Christ, the church "came of age" and now no longer needs the Civil Law to instruct her on the true nature of sin. The death of Christ upon the cross, whereon He suffered the wrath of God against the sin of His people, is more than sufficient to serve this purpose.

The Apostle Paul uses this analogy of growth and development in Galatians when he explains the relationship of the Mosaic Law (circumcision in particular) to the life of the New Covenant believer. In Galatians 3:24-26, Paul writes that the Mosaic Law was Israel's "guardian until Christ came, in order that we might be justified by faith. But now that faith has come, we are no longer under a guardian, for in Christ Jesus you are all sons of God, through faith." The Greek word, *paidagōgos*, can be translated "guardian, pedagogue, child tender, or tutor." Paul's word choice indicates that he viewed the church under the Old Covenant like an immature child in need of a tutor. The Civil Law performed the duties of a tutor in disciplining, instructing, and preparing the church for the coming of Jesus Christ in the incarnation. Paul expands this analogy in Galatians 4:1-5 and speaks of the Old Covenant church like an heir who was not yet mature enough to manage his inheritance and so was put under the care of guardians and managers until the time appointed by his father. The guardian was the Mosaic Law and the appointed time, Paul says, was when "God sent forth his Son, born of woman, born under the law, to redeem those who were under the law, so that we might receive adoption as sons" (Gal. 4:4b-5).

Why So Severe?
This Pauline analogy is helpful in understanding why the Civil Law in the Old Covenant was so severe and why we don't find that same degree of severity exercised in the discipline of the New Testament church. Why were idolatry and fornication

punishable by death in the Old Covenant but not in the New
Covenant? Was it because God was severe and harsh under the
Old Covenant and has mellowed and become more gracious in
the New Covenant? Of course not! God is no less holy and no
more patient in the New Covenant than He was in the Old. The
reason why the church no longer punishes sin corporeally (i.e.
physically) is because it no longer has the authority to do so.
Under the Old Covenant, the church existed as a spiritual *and*
civil institution, but under the New Covenant that is no longer
the case. The reason why sin is not punished in the same way is
not because God Himself has changed, but because the church
has changed with the passage of time.

Though some may grant this distinction between the
powers of the church and the civil magistrate, they nevertheless
insist that faithful Christians ought to implement the Civil
Law of Israel within their respective nations. Those who are
critical of these movements are sometimes charged with not
loving God's law, being indifferent toward the heinousness of
sin, or being fearful of the unbelieving world's opposition to
such efforts. While there is a kernel of truth to such critiques
(antinomianism and the fear of man are both real problems),
such charges are usually little more than name calling and *ad
hominem* attacks. In the ministry of Christ and the Apostles
(who certainly loved and valued the ministry of Moses!) we
do not find any indication, whether by way of example or
express command, that Christians were expected to establish
and govern every nation under heaven according to the Civil
Law of Israel. Instead, we should look at the Civil Law as the
"rudiments," the "elementary principles" of which Paul spoke
in Galatians 3 that taught the Old Covenant church this simple
truth—the wages of sin is death (Rom. 6:23). Like the colorful
picture books that taught us how to read when we were
children, we should be grateful for the Civil Law and all that

it teaches, but we must look now to the cross whereupon the justice of God is more clearly displayed in the death of Christ.

The Civil Law as a Type

In the *Institutes*, Calvin makes an insightful connection between the land promises of the Old Testament and the future blessings they typified, and the corporeal punishments of the Civil Law and the justice of God that it typified. Of the land promises Calvin writes:

> … in old time, the Lord was pleased to direct the thoughts of His people, and raise their minds to the heavenly inheritance, yet, that their hope might be better maintained, He held it forth, and in a manner, gave a foretaste of it under earthly blessings, whereas the gift of future life, now more clearly and lucidly revealed by the Gospel, leads our minds directly to meditate upon it, the inferior mode of exercise formerly employed to the Jews being now laid aside.[9]

In other words, the Promised Land was meant to be a foretaste of God's greater blessing of the New Heavens and the New Earth. It was a "symbol of the divine benevolence, and a type of the heavenly inheritance" for which the Old Testament saints like Abraham eagerly awaited, "For he was looking forward to the city that has foundations, whose designer and builder is God" (Heb. 11:10).[10] The Promised Land was an aid to the patriarchs' faith, a reassurance that God's promise of a renewed cosmos was true. Calvin sees the same typological significance in the Civil Law and writes of those who:

> … wonder that there is so much variance in God, that those who, in old time, were suddenly visited for their faults with

---

9 Calvin, *Institutes*, 2.11.1.

10 ibid., 2.11.2.

severe and dreadful punishments, He now punishes much more rarely and less severely, as if He laid aside His former anger...But we shall easily disencumber ourselves of such doubts if we attend to that mode of divine administration to which I have adverted—that God was pleased to typify both the gift of future and eternal felicity by terrestrial blessings, *as well as the dreadful nature of spiritual death by bodily punishments,* at that time when He delivered His covenant to the Israelites as under a kind of veil.[11]

Like the blood sacrifices of the Ceremonial Law and the land promises given to Abraham, the bodily punishments of the Civil Law were typological of *spiritual* death, instructive tools to teach Israel that "the soul who sins shall die" (Ezek. 18:4). Christ's earthly ministry communicated this same truth. In His preaching ministry He warned His enemies, "I told you that you would die in your sins, for unless you believe that I am he you will die in your sins" (John 8:24) and through His death upon the cross, Jesus displayed the wrath of God against sin and the fate of all those who reject the good news of the gospel. The Civil Law, rightly understood, shows us the costliness of our sin, but not only that—it also shows the depths of Christ's love in His willingness to pay our debts and reconcile us to the Father!

The Moral Law
Its Everlasting Character
The Moral Law is the absolute, perfect standard of righteousness. It is a perfect and unchangeable standard because it is a reflection of the unchangeably perfect nature and will of God Himself. With God "there is no variation or shadow due to change" (James 1:17). The content and obligation to obey the Moral Law can no sooner change than God can be made to

11 ibid., 2.11.3, emphasis added.

lie, change His mind, or be tempted with evil (Num. 23:19; James 1:13). This law is forever fixed and binding upon all men.

The unique manner in which God delivered the Moral Law in contrast to the way He delivered the Ceremonial and Civil Laws to Israel also reflects their differing levels of importance. God communicated the Ceremonial and Civil Laws to Moses who in turn passed them on to the people. They were communicated through a human intermediary and the medium upon which they were written was vellum or animal skins, items that become brittle and break down with the passage of time. Conversely, God Himself spoke "all these words," all the words of the Ten Commandments (Exod. 20:1), and wrote them with His own finger (Exod. 31:18; 32:16) on tablets of stone. The tablets would not waste away like the perishable vellum, signifying the Moral Law's permanence over and above the Ceremonial and Civil Laws that would pass away in time.

God also commanded Moses to place these tablets in the ark of the covenant (Deut. 10:5) so that Israel would carry them wherever they went as a constant reminder of their duty toward Him. All of these details together indicate that God intended His people to keep the Moral Law forever. It was built to last, made to travel, and uttered by the highest authority possible. What more could He have done to indicate the priority and permanence of the Moral Law?

Its Universal Scope

The Moral Law is binding upon all men because God has made all men. He is the Creator and all men are His creatures. In the same way that the potter has the right to require whatever He desires of the clay (Rom. 9:20-21) so too does God have the right to require obedience of those whom He has made whether they believe in Him or not.

At this point, some may wonder if it is fair for God to require personal, perfect, and perpetual obedience to the Ten Commandments if fallen man is no longer able to offer such obedience. By extension, many believers wonder if they are right to call on and expect their neighbors to abide by the Moral Law even if they are not converted. The twentieth-century Puritan scholar, Ernest Kevan, offers a helpful illustration that answers these questions:

> If a creditor requires his debt of a bankrupt who has wastefully spent everything and made himself unable to pay, what unreasonableness is there in this requirement? It is, therefore, quite irrelevant to bring into the argument such impossibilities as asking men to touch the skies or of commanding blind men to see; for the impossibility under discussion is a moral one, and the impossibility to fulfill the commandment is an impossibility which man has brought upon himself ... It will be seen, therefore, that no degree of human inability to fulfill it can nullify the Law of God or in any way reduce the authority of its claims.[12]

Before the fall, Adam was able to obey the law. It was within his power to obey the Ten Commandments perfectly, to pass the positive test of his obedience, and to inherit eternal life. God was not at fault for "stacking the deck" against man. It was only after Adam's fall that the perfect obedience required became an impossibility. And so, God, in commanding all men to obey His law, is not requiring something of them that is *absolutely* impossible but only *consequentially* impossible due to Adam's sin.

Positive vs. Natural Laws
This enduring quality of the Moral Law over and above the Ceremonial and Civil Laws reflects the Reformed distinction

---

12 Ernest Kevan, *The Moral Law* (Sovereign Grace Publishers, 2001), 56, 59.

between positive and natural laws. Positive, in this context, does not mean laws that are prescriptive ("*Do* this") versus laws that are negative/prohibitive ("*Don't* do this"). That is an important distinction, and one that the Westminster Divines recognize in their exposition of the Ten Commandments. In this context, "positive" refers to those laws that God commanded but could have commanded otherwise and been no less holy in doing so. Take the types of sacrifices offered in the Old Testament as an example. God could have prescribed a different set of ceremonies than He did in the Ceremonial Law and maintained His perfect holiness. He could have commanded that pigs, shellfish, and birds of prey be the acceptable sacrifices. Lambs, bulls, and goats were not intrinsically holy; they were only acceptable because God decided that they should be so. Positive laws find their highest rationale in the sovereign will of God (because He chose to) whereas the highest rationale for the Moral Law is God's nature (because this is a reflection of who He is). John Colquhoun coined a pithy phrase that I always return to when explaining the difference between natural law and positive laws: "The former are 'holy, just, and good,' and therefore they are commanded; the latter are commanded, and therefore they are 'holy, just, and good.'"[13]

This prompts the question—why command positive laws at all? Why didn't God govern mankind according to natural law alone? Ernest Kevan notes that positive laws, because they are not based upon something that man *readily* sees as naturally good or bad, are a better test of his obedience. Of God testing Adam's obedience by the tree of the knowledge of good and evil, Kevan writes: "God purposed, therefore, to try Adam by a positive Law, that in this way the dominion which He had over him might be the more clearly demonstrated. For this reason Adam was not to consider the greatness or the goodness of what was commanded, but merely the will of Him who gave him the

---

13 John Colquhoun, *The Law and the Gospel*, 10.

commandment."[14] By forbidding him to eat of the tree, God was testing whether Adam would obey Him simply because He was God. Had God not tested Adam in this way, Adam, who in his pre-fallen state was inclined to all good, would have kept the Ten Commandments as a simple reflex of his perfect nature—purely out of habit, we might say. But to test his love and submission to God as his King, God required Adam to do something that did not naturally make sense to him. Adam failed that test.

Because He Said So

When thinking through the "whys" of obedience, I have found that the longer I've been a Christian the more content I am with the simple answer, "Because God said so." Whenever a child demands an explanation from his parents for an unpopular decision they've made, that child usually chafes when he hears his parents say, "Because I said so." To the child, it sounds like mom and dad are being capricious, that they don't really have a satisfactory explanation for what they've decided and are appealing to their authority as a trump card. But when we stop and consider the transcendent greatness of God as our authoritative Creator, when we with David say in awestruck wonder "When I look at your heavens, the work of your fingers, the moon and the stars, which you have set in place, what is man that you are mindful of him, and the son of man that you care for him?" (Ps. 8:3-4), then and only then does the explanation, "Because God said so," feel more than satisfactory to us. "God says so" is enough by itself to require obedience to the Moral Law. But praise be to God that there are countless other reasons why believers should obey God's commands, chief among them being the love and mercy shown to us in Jesus Christ.

---

14 Ernest Kevan, *The Moral Law,* 50.

The Moral Law Clarified

"Which Is the Greatest Commandment?"

One of the chief signs of mastery is the ability to make the complex simple. It doesn't take an expert to explain a difficult concept in a heady, esoteric manner. Regurgitating facts does not mean that one actually *understands* those facts. But, when a physicist, mathematician, or auto-mechanic is able to distill vast sums of information so that people like me (who are abysmal at all things numerical and mechanical) can understand, this demonstrates that the expert understands his field of study thoroughly enough to distinguish between matters of primary and secondary importance.

Jesus had such a mastery of the law of God—a perfect mastery. We see this on display in the simple, straight-forward answer He gave to a Pharisee's difficult question: "And one of them, a lawyer, asked him a question to test him. 'Teacher, which is the greatest commandment in the Law?'" (Matt. 22:35-36). Behind the lawyer's question was a desire to put Jesus in His place, to prove that this carpenter from Galilee was no match for the learning of the Jewish establishment. But the lawyer's plan backfired royally, because not only did Christ tell him which commandment was the greatest, He told him what the second great commandment was to boot: "And he said to him, 'You shall love the Lord your God with all your heart and with all your soul and with all your mind. This is the great and first commandment. And a second is like it: You shall love your neighbor as yourself. On these two commandments depend all the Law and the Prophets'" (Matt. 22:37-40; cf. Mark. 12:28-31).

Horizontal and Vertical Commandments

The first and greatest commandment is a direct quotation of Deuteronomy 6:5. When read in light of the *Shema*, the great statement of Yahweh's unique status as the only true God in verse 4, one can hear an implied "therefore" before the "You shall" of verse 5. "Hear, O Israel: The Lord our God, the Lord is one. You shall love the Lord your God with all your heart and with all your soul and with all your might" (Deut. 6:4-5). God being the only true God establishes Him as the only fitting object of our love and devotion. If through Him and Him alone, "we live and move and have our being" then it is only logical that He should be our all in all. The whole of our lives, our minds, our wills, our affections, and our worship are to be oriented toward Him who loved us and sent His only begotten Son to die for our sins (John 3:16). This first and greatest commandment to love God encapsulates the first four commandments of the Decalogue (i.e. the first table). Together they show us *how* to love God with all our hearts. Because their focus is primarily Godward, we will refer to them as our vertical duties.

The second greatest commandment is first expressed in Leviticus 19:18: "You shall not take vengeance or bear a grudge against the sons of your own people, but you shall love your neighbor as yourself: I am the Lord" (cf. Lev. 19:34). This commandment is at the heart of Jesus' golden rule in the

Sermon on the Mount, where He says: "So whatever you wish that others would do to you, do also to them, for this is the Law and the Prophets" (Matt. 7:12). The primary focus of these latter six commandments (i.e. second table) is on how we treat one another. For that reason, we will call them our horizontal duties. As we make this distinction, we mustn't lose sight of the fact that there is often a degree of overlap between the two tables. Horizontal sins *always* have a vertical dimension inherent in them and vertical sins *can* and often do involve sinning against our neighbors.[1]

Going Deeper

The remainder of this chapter will examine each commandment using the Westminster Larger and Shorter Catechisms as helpful guides. One of the most convicting and illuminating features of their breakdown of the Ten Commandments is the recognition that on the flip side of every prohibition is an implicit prescription. The Larger Catechism teaches, "Where a duty is commanded, the contrary sin is forbidden, and, where a sin is forbidden, the contrary duty is commanded: so where a promise is annexed, the contrary threatening is included: and, where a threatening is annexed, the contrary promise is included" (WLC Q.99).[2] While it may sound like the Divines are reading more into the Ten Commandments than is actually there, ask yourself—when God calls us away from sin, what is He calling us *to*? Righteousness. In the same way that Paul warned the Galatians against the works of the flesh (Gal. 5:19-20) and immediately transitioned to their polar opposite in commending the fruit of the Spirit (Gal. 5:22-24) so too are the Divines showing us that righteousness is more than simply refraining from sin but embracing all that God commands.

---

1 See Appendix 2.

2 cf. Calvin's *Institutes* 2.8.8, 9.

The First Commandment

You shall have no other gods before me ...
—Exodus 20:3

The first commandment governs what or whom we worship.[3]
In Isaiah 44:6, we are reminded that the LORD is the "King
of Israel and his Redeemer, the LORD of hosts: 'I am the first
and I am the last; besides me there is no god." This, like the
Shema, is a clear statement of monotheism—there is only one
true God and so He is the only one we are to worship. What
then are we to make of the "no other gods before me" in the
first commandment? At first reading it may sound like God
is acknowledging: one, the existence of other gods; and two,
that so long as He is first in line we are free to worship lesser
gods beside Him. But this is not the case. The "gods" of the first
commandment are gods in name only—they are idols: not real,
incapable of salvation, and bringing destruction upon all who
worship them (Ps. 115:4-8).

The prohibition to not have any other gods "before me" means
that God, by virtue of His omnipresence and omniscience,

---

3 It is worth noting here that Lutherans and Presbyterians differ in the way
that they number the Ten Commandments. According to the Lutheran
order, the first commandment forbids idolatry, the second forbids taking
God's name in vain, the ninth forbids coveting your neighbor's wife, and
the tenth coveting your neighbor's possessions. The textual argument
that I find most persuasive in favor of the Reformed view is the inverted
order of the commandments forbidding covetousness in Exodus 20:17 and
Deuteronomy 5:21. In Exodus 20, when God delivered the Ten Commandments, the order was "You shall not covet your neighbor's house; you shall
not covet your neighbor's wife..." But, in Deuteronomy 5, the word order
is reversed by Moses, "You shall not covet your neighbor's wife. And you
shall not desire your neighbor's house...". If the prohibitions against coveting
your neighbor's wife and coveting your neighbor's house are distinct
commandments, then which is the ninth and which is the tenth? Should we
follow Exodus or Deuteronomy's order? The easiest explanation is to treat
both prohibitions against covetousness as one commandment, which is the
Reformed position.

sees and hates all idols whether fashioned with our hands or cherished in our hearts. Though we may never have physically bowed down to and worshipped a statue of wood or stone, we are still guilty of breaking the first commandment. Even our secret sins are *coram Deo,* before the face of God.

The first commandment expressly forbids the worshipping of false gods, but it extends even further and forbids loving the good things of life to an inordinately high degree. Our temptation upon receiving good gifts from God is to love and cherish them over and above their giver. Good and lawful things like family, friends, work, and our homes actually have the *greatest* potential of becoming idols. As Thomas Watson said so picturesquely, "More are hurt by excess in lawful things than by meddling with unlawful, as more are killed by wine than poison."[4] Good things can subtly morph and become ultimate things if we do not vigilantly guard our hearts against idolatry. Like Israel whom Moses warned as they were about to enter the land flowing with milk and honey, we must be careful not to forget God whose goodness and beauty far outshine even the greatest pleasures of this life (Deut. 6:10-15).

The only way to displace the sin of idolatry is to replace it with love for Jesus Christ. Thomas Chalmers called this the expulsive power of a new affection. Like a nail that is hammered into a log to dislodge another nail that is sunk deep into the wood, the love of Christ is the only way to drive the love of idols from our hearts. It all starts with simply looking to Christ in saving faith. When we see Him as He is, then, as Helen Lemmel wrote, "the things of earth will grow strangely dim in the light of His glory and grace."[5] The first commandment tells us to turn away from beholding vain things and to turn our eyes upon Jesus instead.

---

4 Thomas Watson, *The Duty of Self-Denial and 10 Other Sermons: By Thomas Watson* (Morgan, PA: Soli Deo Gloria Publications, 1996), 15.

5 From the hymn "Turn Your Eyes upon Jesus" by Helen Lemmel.

The Second Commandment

> *You shall not make for yourself a carved image ...*
> —Exodus 20:4-6

If the first commandment forbids offering worship to anyone or anything but God, then the second commandment forbids worshipping God in any way that He has not revealed in His Word. Stated positively, the second commandment requires that we worship the right God in the right way.

At face value, the second commandment forbids making and worshipping any physical representation of any persons of the triune God. Because God is a "most pure spirit, invisible, without body, parts" (WCF 2.1) and the Creator of all things, it is contrary to His very nature to use a physical, created object for personal devotion, discipleship, or in corporate worship. It is beneath His transcendent dignity. Voltaire famously said, "In the beginning God created man in His own image, and man has been trying to repay the favor ever since." Though no friend of biblical Christianity, Voltaire was on to something—image-making effectively reverses the Creator-creature distinction. We need not make any image of Christ because we already have one—*we* are made in His image.

The earliest example of God's displeasure with object worship is seen in the infamous golden calf incident in Exodus 32. Over the course of the forty days that Moses was enveloped in the cloud on Mt. Sinai, the people grew antsy. They were tired of living by faith—they wanted to live by sight. In their impatience they commanded Aaron, "Up, make us gods who shall go before us. As for this Moses, the man who brought us up out of the land of Egypt, we do not know what has become of him" (Exod. 32:1). Aaron complied and took the gold given to him by the people and fashioned the golden calf. Though some argue that the mention of "gods" in verses 1 and 4 proves that Israel's sin was a transgression of the first commandment (i.e. polytheism) and not the second commandment, Aaron's instructions in verses 4 and 5 indicate that Israel intended to worship their covenant LORD using the golden calf, "And Aaron made a proclamation and said, 'Tomorrow shall be a feast to the LORD'" (cf. Neh. 9:18).[6]

God's swift judgment upon the people's false worship (Exod. 32:27-28) serves as a solemn reminder that special revelation, not the human imagination, is the arbiter of what is and is not permissible in worship. Worship must always be by the Book. Consider too the example of Nadab and Abihu in Leviticus 10:1-2:

> Now Nadab and Abihu, the sons of Aaron, each took his censer and put fire in it and laid incense on it and offered unauthorized fire before the Lord, which he had not commanded them. And fire came out from before the Lord and consumed them, and they died before the Lord.

Moses says that Nadab and Abihu offered "unauthorized fire" or, as the King James Version puts it, "strange fire." Lest the reader interpret the word "unauthorized" to mean the same thing as forbidden, verse 1 says explicitly, "which He had not commanded them." Nadab and Abihu were not struck down because they approached God in a way that He had *forbidden*; they were struck down because they approached Him in a manner other than He had *commanded*. Instead of being creative, Nadab and Abihu should have been submissive

---

6 In Hebrew, the term used for "gods" in verses 1 and 4 is *Elohim*. *Elohim* can refer either to "gods" (plural) or as a divine name for the one true God. When this plural noun form is applied to a singular noun in Hebrew it is called a plural of excellence or majesty. Another example of the plural of majesty is Proverbs 9:10 where the word for "Holy One" is plural, not singular: "The fear of the LORD is the beginning of wisdom, and the knowledge of the Holy One is insight."

to what God had previously revealed about the proper way to approach Him. The reason why God does not punish unauthorized worship today with the same severity as He did in these instances has been dealt with already in the previous chapter. It is worth reiterating here that God is no less holy under the New Covenant than He was under the Old. God still cares about the way He is worshipped, and His people should take great care to search the Scriptures and learn how to worship God in a manner that pleases *Him*.

The Third Commandment

You shall not take the name of the LORD your God in vain …
—Exodus 20:7

My first exposure to expository preaching was a sermon series on the names of God. Never before had I stopped to consider the many names of God in Scripture and the rich truths they communicate about Him, names like *Elohim*, *El Elyon* ("God Most High," Gen. 14:19), *Yahweh* or *Jehovah* ("I Am Who I Am," Exod. 3:14), *Jehovah Jireh* ("The Lord Will Provide," Gen. 22:14), and *Jehovah Sabaoth* ("The Lord of Hosts," 1 Sam. 1:3). What those sermons taught me was that God's names are not aspirational like so many of our own. (What else could explain the presence of so many Calvins, Knoxs, and Owens in Presbyterian and Reformed churches!) They are revelational, a window through which we behold God as He is. This means that whenever we use God's name in a careless manner, we are treating God Himself in a careless way.

Scripture teaches that the words of our mouths are a reflection of our hearts (Luke 6:45). Irreverent words betray an irreverent attitude of heart and mind. True as this is, however, it is also possible to succumb to the same duplicity that marked the people of God in Isaiah's day and the Pharisees in Christ's: "This people honors me with their lips, but their heart is far from me; in vain do they worship me, teaching as doctrines the commandments of men" (Matt. 15:8-9). The words of our mouths and the mediations of our hearts ought always to agree that God is holy and worthy of praise (Ps. 19:14).

Revelation Is Personal

Blaspheming God's name (Lev. 24:11), using it in an empty manner, or as a way to add *gravitas* to our personal opinion ("God told me that we should do …") are all ways in which we break the third commandment. But there is far more to it: the commandment's concern is not just with the reverent use of God's revelatory names but with all the ways in which He reveals Himself to man. As the Shorter Catechism says, "The Third Commandment forbiddeth all profaning or abusing *anything* whereby God taketh Himself known" (WSC Q. 55, emphasis mine). This includes His names, titles (e.g. Lord, Christ, Messiah), attributes (omniscience, omnipresence, omnipotence, love, justice, holiness, etc…), ordinances (e.g. the Lord's Supper and baptism), Word, and works (e.g. God's work of creation, Christ's miracles, etc… see WSC Q. 54). Revelation, in other words, is personal—it is nothing less than divine self-disclosure. Whether in the heavens above or in the Word in our hands, God is speaking to us and we must pay close attention to all that He says.

Hallowing God's Name

In the Sermon on the Mount Jesus gave His disciples a perfect model for prayer. The Lord's Prayer opens with the petition "Our Father in heaven, hallowed be your name" (Matt. 6:9). Jesus is asking the Father to maintain the sacredness of His name throughout the world; His chief concern is that the Father's name would be glorified in all things. Jesus commanded His disciples to "Pray then like this" (Matt. 6:9), and by His own example showed them what it meant to live for the glory of the Father's name—to live obediently to His will in all things. God's name is hallowed whenever we do His will on earth with the same readiness with which the angels do His will in heaven (Matt. 6:10). God's name is hallowed whenever we are insulted and suffer for the name of Christ (1 Pet. 4:14). God's name is hallowed whenever a sinner calls upon the name of the Lord and is saved (Acts 2:21). His name is the name above all names, and so His people are to honor it in all that they do.

The Fourth Commandment

Remember the Sabbath day, to keep it holy …
—Exodus 20:8-11

The Origin of the Sabbath Day
Why did the God who "does not faint or grow weary" (Isa. 40:28) rest on the seventh day? Clearly it was not out of necessity—Genesis 2 does not say that God *needed* to rest. No, God rested, ceasing from His work of creation, because He knew that finite man would need to rest from his work. When God sanctified the Sabbath, making it holy, the wellbeing of all who bear His image was at the forefront of His mind: "The Sabbath was made for man, not man for the Sabbath" (Mark 2:27).

Forgetting the Sabbath Day
One of the many reasons for the covenant peoples' exile to Babylon was its disregard for the Sabbath day. In Jeremiah 17:19-27, the prophet is commanded to stand at the People's Gate and to say to the people of Judah, "Take care for the sake of your lives, and do not bear a burden on the Sabbath day or bring it by the gates of Jerusalem" (v. 21). How did they respond? "Yet they did not listen or incline their ear, but stiffened their neck, that they might not hear and receive instruction" (v. 23). They doubled down on their sin and chose to serve the almighty dollar instead of Almighty God. It didn't have to be this way, but for their

transgression God promised to kindle a fire in Jerusalem's gates that would "devour the palaces of Jerusalem" (v. 27). God cared about how His people treated the Sabbath day, but the people, by and large, couldn't have cared less. They had more important matters to attend to.

In the New Testament, we see the exact opposite problem. The Pharisees for their part, agonized over the minutest details of Sabbath keeping. Their sin was losing the forest for the trees. So fixated had they become upon their many man-made traditions and commandments that when Jesus' disciples plucked heads of grain in the field on the Sabbath, the Pharisees charged them with unlawful labor (Matt. 12:2). And if that weren't bad enough, when Jesus healed the invalid of thirty-eight years in John 5, the Pharisees, instead of rejoicing over the man's recovery and Jesus' divine power, rebuked the invalid saying, "It is the Sabbath, and it is not lawful for you to take up your bed…Who is the man who said to you, 'Take up your bed, and walk'?" (John 5:10-12). They didn't care that the man had been healed. They wanted to know, "Who told you that you could break our rules?" The Pharisees had lost the plot; they had forgotten that God desires mercy, and not sacrifice (Matt. 12:7). It always was and is lawful to do good to our neighbor on the Sabbath (Matt. 12:9-14).

Israel transgressed the Sabbath day in the Old Testament by way of disregard and in the New Testament the Pharisees failed to keep the Sabbath by making burdensome that which was meant to be a blessing. One can miss the Sabbath through carelessness *and* an unbecoming carefulness. We must beware of both extremes.

Remembering the Sabbath Day

How, then, do we sanctify and remember the Sabbath? The Shorter Catechism asks this same question (Q. 60) and gives us a helpful answer:

... by a holy resting, even from such worldly enjoyments and recreations as are lawful on other days; and spending the whole time in the public and private exercises of God's worship, except so much as is to be taken up in the works of necessity and mercy.

In summary, the Standards emphasize that the whole day ought to be spent in public and private worship, morning and evening singing praises to our God (Ps. 92:1-3), and ceasing from other recreations.[7] Worship is the means whereby we attain the *spiritual* rest that God holds out to us on this day.

The debate over this commandment typically lies in discussions about "worldly recreations." Whether it be a desire not to cook on Sunday afternoons, or watching sports as a means to relax and enjoy time with loved ones, there is the temptation to engage in things which, on any other day of the week, would be perfectly sensible and acceptable. I hear the concern, applaud the desire to spend time with loved ones, and understand the need for physical rest—we are all human! And yet the Sabbath, made for man, was designed and defined by God—and He calls us to rest from all worldly recreations for our good and the good of our neighbor. The barista, the waitress, the professional athlete, and the movie theater ticket-taker all have a divinely-given right to Sabbath rest. We cannot deprive our neighbor of his rest in the interest of pursuing our own. Remembering the Sabbath day is a means of loving God and loving neighbor—but since no two people apply the

---

7   We must not respond to God's "challenging a special propriety" (WLC Q. 120) in the Sabbath day with the same begrudging attitude with which Adam and Eve responded to His forbidding them to eat of the tree of the knowledge of good and evil. They had every other tree available to them in the Garden and only one tree that God said "This is not for you." God has given us six days for work and recreation and so we should not resent Him for setting aside just one whole day for His worship.

Scriptures in the exact same way, a good question to ask is: Is what I am about to do going to enhance or inhibit my and my neighbor's ability to rest and worship on this day?[8]

The key to delighting in the Sabbath day is to stop thinking of it in exclusively privative terms. The Sabbath is not about what we don't get to do; it's about what we get to do. Sundays are the church's weekly honeymoon with her Savior. We are Christ's bride and He is our bridegroom. If on my honeymoon I had been glued to my cellphone, disappeared to watch the big game, and was engaged in the endless back and forth of work emails, my wife would have been understandably displeased. Why? Not because cellphones, sports, or email are bad in themselves, but because they would have distracted me from the purpose of my honeymoon—being with my wife! On the Sabbath, God clears His calendar to make time to be with His people and so His people should, in turn, clear their calendars to commune with and rest in Him.

---

8 Of course, there are necessary matters that must be attended to in order to sanctify the Sabbath day. As a minister, Sunday is a day of work for me. And yet, because it enables me and my neighbors to rest and worship on the Sabbath, I am not just permitted but *required* to perform my duties heartily as unto the Lord (cf. Matt. 12:5). The same goes for those who labor in life-saving occupations (e.g. police officers, doctors, nurses, etc.) and who show mercy to those in need (e.g. homeless shelters, soup kitchens, etc.). This principle of necessity extends all the way down to practical matters of the home as well. Families need to eat on the Lord's Day, so food preparation is a necessity. Developmentally, children need to run and play to burn off energy (especially if they are coming back for evening worship!). I, personally, am a big proponent of a Sunday afternoon nap. God cares about our souls *and* our bodies, and anything necessary to maintain our bodies so that we can worship is permitted on the Lord's Day. For more guidance on Sabbath observance, see: Joseph Pipa, *The Lord's Day* (Fearn: Christian Focus, 2013); Walter Chantry *Call The Sabbath A Delight* (Edinburgh: The Banner of Truth, 1991); and, Ryan McGraw, *The Day of Worship* (Grand Rapids: Reformation Heritage Books, 2015).

The Fifth Commandment

> *Honor your father and your mother …*
> —Exodus 20:12

"Can't live with it, can't live without it." Such is the attitude of many toward authority in this life. All of us are under one form of authority or another, whether in the home, in the world, or in the church (not to mention God's authority over us as Creator). Authority is inescapable. Hence it is most fitting that the first commandment that deals with our horizontal duties toward others teaches us how to respond appropriately to authority.

Authority: Intrinsically Good or Evil?

Many negative attitudes toward authority arise out of a fundamental misunderstanding of its origin and purpose. After Adam and Eve fell into sin, God said to the woman, "Your desire shall be contrary to your husband, but he shall rule over you" (Gen. 3:16). That the first mention of one human being ruling another is found after the fall, some argue, is proof positive that authority is intrinsically evil. Like the physical consequences of painful childbearing and toilsome labor amidst thorns and thistles, authority is seen as punishment for Adam and Eve's eating the forbidden fruit. Eve's desire would be contrary to her husband and Adam in turn would rule over his wife with a dictatorial, iron fist. Whether one maintains this negative interpretation of "rule over you" in Genesis 3, or, like me, sees it as a simple statement of fact makes no difference.[9] The mere mention of "rule" after the fall does not mean that Adam did not exercise authority *prior* to the fall. The most that can be said from Genesis 3:16 is that authority, like the Moral Law written on Adam and Eve's hearts, was subject to corruption and manipulation after sin entered into the world.

---

9 I take Genesis 3:16 to mean that Eve's desire would be to usurp her husband's authority, but, nevertheless, Adam would continue as her covenant head (cf. Eph. 5:23).

From the Cradle to the Cubicle
The fifth commandment takes us back to the proving grounds where we learn the art of joyful submission for the first time—the nuclear family. It is in the home that children first learn that "there is no authority except from God" (Rom. 13:1) and that obedience is right and pleasing in the sight of the Lord (Eph. 6:1; Col. 3:20). Chances are that if a child resists the loving correction and tender guidance of his parents in the home, he will be equally if not more resistant to authority in every other area of life. On the other hand, if a child does heed his father's instruction and keeps his mother's teaching, then he will be more inclined to obey other earthly authorities (Prov. 1:8, 22:6). One could call this trickle-down obedience; submission to authority begins in the home, but by no means is it meant to end there. As Larger Catechism 124 teaches, the language of "father and mother" is shorthand for all who are or will be authorities over us in this life.

Honor Swings Both Ways
Though the express wording of the commandment deals with the responsibilities of inferiors to their superiors, Larger Catechism 129 lists a handful of the many ways that superiors are to honor their inferiors in accordance with the fifth commandment—they are to love, pray for, bless, commend, correct, and provide all things needful for their souls.[10] We are all too prone to forget this. Even Jesus' own disciples needed to be reminded "that the rulers of the Gentiles lord it over them, and their great ones exercise authority over them. It shall not be so among you" (Matt. 20:25, 26a).

In Paul's letters, for every command to inferiors there is a corresponding command issued to superiors. When wives

---

10 By "superior" and "inferior" the Divines were speaking relationally, not ontologically (in terms of being). They meant the same thing we do when we say in the workplace, "I will need to run that by my superiors."

are told to submit to their husbands, husbands are told to love their wives and "not be harsh with them" (Col. 3:18, 19). When children are commanded to obey their parents, fathers are warned not to provoke their children to anger (Eph. 6:1, 4). When bondservants are exhorted to render service to their earthly masters with good will, masters are reminded to "do the same to them" (Eph. 6:5, 9). All parties are duty-bound to honor one another.

The best example of authority rightly exercised is seen nowhere better than in the life of Jesus Christ. Christ came in the incarnation "not to be served but to serve, and to give his life as a ransom for many" (Matt. 20:28). Though He was in the form of God, He did not "count equality with God a thing to be grasped, but emptied himself, by taking the form of a servant, being born in the likeness of men" (Phil. 2:6-7). If Christ, who has been given all authority in heaven and on earth, used His authority to serve His people, then so too must we treat authority as a means of benefiting those around us.

The Sixth Commandment

You shall not murder ...
—Exodus 20:13

The Moral Law is spiritual, meaning its demands penetrate to the level of our understanding, will, affections, and all other powers of the soul (WLC Q. 99:2). In the Sermon on the Mount, Jesus unearthed this deeper, spiritual dimension of the Moral Law and cleared away centuries of misinterpretation that had been popularized by the scribes and Pharisees. Many men went to that sermon believing they were faultless concerning the law, but none who truly listened that day could walk away without knowing that they were guilty of breaking the sixth commandment. Jesus said to the crowds:

> You have heard that it was said to those of old, "You shall not murder; and whoever murders will be liable to judgment." But I say to you that everyone who is angry with his brother will be liable to judgment; whoever insults his brother will be liable to the council; and whoever says, "You fool!" will be liable to the hell of fire (Matt. 5:21, 22).

Destroying Life

The Pharisees mistakenly believed that the sixth commandment only forbade the unjust taking of another person's life. Their religious caste was the one who "said of old" that the commandment was limited to literal murder only. But Jesus proved this was not the case by revealing to them something deeper than the mere letter of the law. Using the sixth and seventh commandments as examples, Jesus established the interpretive principle that where the Moral Law condemns the *fruit* of sin it also condemns the *root* of sin.[11]

Before Cain killed his brother Abel, Cain "was very angry, and his face fell" (Gen. 4:5). God confronted Cain in his anger asking, "Why are you angry, and why has your face fallen?" (v. 6) because God knew that if Cain did not rule over his sinful anger, it would soon rule over him (v. 7). Had Cain mortified his anger before it came to full bloom in that bloody field, Abel's life would have been spared and Cain would not have been consigned to a cursed life of wandering upon the earth. God treats all forms of murder as deadly, even murder committed in the heart.

Jesus' Sermon on the Mount also classifies hurtful speech under the umbrella of murder. Proverbs 12:18 says, "There is one whose rash words are like sword thrusts, but the tongue of the wise brings healing." Words inflict real damage, but they can also promote tremendous good. Who hasn't been edified by a

---

11 See WLC Q. 99:5.

well-timed word of encouragement from a Christian brother or sister? Words are powerful, and the sixth commandment requires that we use them well. Before we speak, we need to ask ourselves, "Am I using my words for the purpose of building up or tearing down?"

Promoting Life

On the flip side of the sixth commandment's forbidding the sin of murder in all its forms (attitudinal, verbal, and physical) is the requirement to do everything in our power to protect and promote the wellbeing of our neighbor. We are commanded to do for him what we would want him to do for us. This is true religion at work. Christians ought to be models of what it means to live justly and to love mercy (Micah 6:8), we are to "do good to everyone, and especially to those who are of the household of faith" (Gal. 6:10). In his first epistle, John calls on his readers to love not in word or talk but in deed and in truth (1 John 3:18). Talk is cheap, but real love is costly. We are required and compelled to love in this way because that is how our Savior loved us—He told us of His love and He showed us His love through His substitutionary death upon the cross. Jesus meant what *He* said and so should it be with our love toward our neighbor—we must love in word *and* in action.

The Seventh Commandment

> *You shall not commit adultery ...*
> —Exodus 20:14

If you flip on the news and see a crowd of pro-choice protesters holding up their picket signs, chances are there will be a handful emblazoned with the words "My body, my choice." That is the thinking that underlies the entire abortion industry and the sexual immorality that constantly feeds it—that our bodies belong only to ourselves. According to such an autonomous way of thinking, sex is viewed as little more than an itch to scratch, a physical craving that we are free to satisfy however, whenever, and with whomever we like. Scripture, on the other hand, holds the dignity of the body and human sexuality in much higher esteem.

This commandment requires all to live chastely by avoiding lustful thoughts, crude conversation, and to abstain from all sexual activity outside of marriage. This is not because sex is somehow dirty or defiling, but because our bodies are fearfully and wonderfully made and because sex is a precious gift given by God for the purpose of procreation and strengthening the marriage bond. The great rationale undergirding this commandment is the counter-cultural truth that we are not our own. We belong, body and soul, to God. Obeying the seventh commandment, then, is a matter of stewarding our bodies for the glory of the One to whom we belong.

Desperate Measures

As He did with the sixth commandment, Jesus identifies lustful intent as a species of adultery much to the surprise of the Pharisees. Some today interpret Matthew 5:28 to mean that Jesus was teaching that adultery in the heart is equally as heinous as adultery committed with the body, but that is not what Jesus meant. Committing adultery physically is objectively worse than doing so only mentally (WSC Q. 83, WLC Q. 151.3). Remember, Jesus was not speaking to men who believed that lust wasn't *that* sinful—He was speaking to men who didn't believe it was sinful at all! This is why He speaks of lust with such solemnity and calls it adultery in the heart, it was to shake His hearers from their spiritual stupor and to warn them that lust, even if it doesn't result in physical adultery, was still a condemnable sin in God's sight.

Jesus says that there are no measures too radical to deal with lust. The Christian must kill lust or his lust will be killing him.[12] Speaking figuratively, Jesus declares:

> If your right eye causes you to sin, tear it out and throw it away. For it is better that you lose one of your members than that your whole body be thrown into hell. And if your right hand causes you to sin, cut it off and throw it away. For it is better that you lose one of your members than that your whole body go into hell. (Matt. 5:29-30)

Because most people are right-hand and right-eye dominant (sorry lefties!), the image of tearing out one's right eye and cutting off their right hand conveys the necessity of setting aside anything, however precious, for the sake of obeying Christ. Painful and inconvenient as it would be to live the rest of my life without my right eye or right hand, if doing so meant that the rest of my body would be spared from premature death, I would consider the sacrifice well worth it. Like the American mountaineer Aron Lee Ralston, who famously broke and amputated his own arm with a dull pocketknife to free himself from a dislodged boulder, so too must the Christian be willing to part with anything in this life in order to avoid temptations to sin (cf. Matt. 18:7-9). Sometimes this will require that we find a new group of friends. Other times it will demand that we abstain from certain forms of entertainment or technology for a time, or perhaps indefinitely. Obedience is costly, but the value of our immortal souls more than justifies the expense (Mark 8:36).

---

12 This is an adaptation of John Owen's famous line, "Be killing sin or it will be killing you."

The Eighth Commandment

> *You shall not steal …*
> —Exodus 20:15

When you think of theft what images come most immediately to mind? Perhaps you think of corrupt businessmen like Bernie Maydoff who embezzled tens of millions of dollars from his clients. Or if you grew up in the era of the iPod like I did, you remember how popular it was to download songs for free from websites like Napster and LimeWire instead of paying for them on the iTunes store. Theft has many different forms, but all of them involve either taking away or withholding from our neighbor anything that rightly belongs to him.

Stealing via Commission

When Adam and Eve took and ate the forbidden fruit, they became the world's first thieves—an Edenic Bonnie and Clyde. Following in their forefather's footsteps, men like Achan who hid the devoted things under his tent (Josh. 7:10-26), King David who stole his close friend's wife, Bathsheba (2 Sam. 11), and Ahab who had Naboth killed in order to steal his vineyard (1 Kings 21), all actively *took* something or someone that did not belong to them.

Theft, as we ordinarily think of it, is against someone else. We take something from someone. But, as the Larger Catechism teaches, it is also possible to steal from ourselves. Among the sins forbidden in the eighth commandment are, "idleness, prodigality, wasteful gaming; and all other ways whereby we do unduly prejudice our own outward estate, and defrauding ourselves of the due use and comfort of that estate which God hath given us" (WLC Q. 142).

In the book of Proverbs, we have the preeminent example of how laziness leads to ruin in the life of the sluggard: "The sluggard does not plow in the autumn; he will seek at the harvest and have nothing" (Prov. 20:4). The sluggard through his laziness robbed himself of the peace and security that would have been his if he'd been willing to set his hand to the plow and work. His field, with its broken-down wall and thorns and nettles covering the ground, serve as a warning that if we rest when we ought to work, poverty will come upon us "like a robber, and want like an armed man" (Prov. 6:11). When we are lazy, we become our own worst enemies.

Stealing via Omission

In June 2023, Business Insider featured an article titled, "A Gen Xer Who Secretly Works 3-Full Time Remote Jobs and Makes \$344,000 Paid Off His Mortgage and Is Saving to Send His Kids to College Debt-Free."[13] What a title. Joseph, a forty-eight-year-old network engineer, was in the process of leaving one full-time remote working job to start another when a colleague floated the idea of Joseph working both jobs simultaneously without his employers knowing it. Joseph agreed and later added a third job, again, without telling any of his employers. The article reads, "At first, Joseph said, his wife was not a fan of him working multiple jobs and thought it was morally wrong. But he persisted and said his wife was now OK with him deciding how long he would continue this lifestyle."[14] Joseph should have listened to his wife—what he was doing was morally wrong—as Joseph's sin required him to lie to each of his employers (ninth commandment) and to work fewer hours than they expected him to.

---

13 Jacob Zinkula, "A Gen Xer Who Secretly Works 3-Full Time Remote Jobs and Makes \$344,000 Paid Off His Mortgage and Is Saving to Send His Kids to College Debt-Free," *Entrepreneur.com* from *Business Insider*, June 22, 2023, https://www.entrepreneur.com/business-news/man-secretly-works-3-full-time-remote-jobs-earns-344k/454637.

14 ibid.

Omissive theft happens whenever we unjustly withhold something that is due to another. When we cheat on our taxes, we are robbing Caesar of the money that is due to him (Luke 20:25). Workaholics deprive their spouse and children of the quality time that they deserve when they are constantly at the office or glued to their cellphone. When Christians refuse to tithe their income, they are robbing their local church of the material resources needed to support the work of the ministry (1 Cor. 9:11) and they are robbing God of the first fruits He is due (Prov. 3:9-10).

In Deuteronomy 22:4 Moses commands, "You shall not see your brother's donkey or his ox fallen down by the way and ignore them. You shall help him to lift them up again." Refusing to help alleviate our neighbor's physical needs when it is within our power to do so also violates the eighth commandment. That is essentially what the priest and Levite did in the parable of the Good Samaritan when they hurried by their bloodied kinsman; they deprived him of the physical healing and care he needed.

Sharing Our Blessings

If the eighth commandment forbids taking or withholding that which is not ours, then it requires that we give generously and joyously. Paul embodies the spirit of Large Catechism 99:4 ("where a sin is forbidden, the contrary duty is commanded") in Ephesians 4:28: "Let the thief no longer steal, but rather let him labor, doing honest work with his own hands, so that he may have something to share with anyone in need." Instead of stealing from others (or ourselves), God's people are to labor industriously and prosperously, so prosperously that we have something to share with the poor. Admittedly, most of us are motivated to work because we know that it provides for the needs of our families. This is a right motivation (1 Tim. 5:8), but it should not be our only motivation. In the New Testament believers were eager to supply for each other's needs (Acts 2:44-45). Paul reminded the church in Corinth that the Lord loves a cheerful giver (2 Cor. 9:7). This same joy ought to mark our own hearts whenever we give. We should count it our joy and privilege to be the means whereby God keeps His promise to give His people their daily bread (Ps. 37:25; Matt. 6:11).

The Ninth Commandment

You shall not bear false witness against your neighbor ...
—Exodus 20:16

The sin of bearing false witness in a court of law is the representative sin of the ninth commandment because it is extremely damaging to the offended party, in some cases mortally so. Christ Himself was subject to such false witnesses on the night when the Sanhedrin tried Him in their kangaroo court: "For many bore false witness against him, but their testimony did not agree" (Mark 14:56). The saying we learn as children "Sticks and stones may break my bones, but words will never hurt me" rings hollow when we read passages like this. Few of us will ever be called to testify in court, but we are all called to bear witness to the truth in ordinary matters of life.

Gossip is a serious sin, regardless of how "respectable" we have made it.[15] It is so serious that in Romans 1 Paul says that it is characteristic of those whom God has given up to a debased mind and who do what ought not to be done (Rom. 1:29). The typical reason that we gossip and slander is because we want to exercise control over our neighbor. We want to bring him low and to raise ourselves up. The ninth commandment, however, requires us to love, desire, and rejoice in our neighbor's good

---

15 See Jerry Bridges's excellent book *Respectable Sins* (Colorado Springs: NavPress, 2007).

name instead. This means covering over their infirmities and freely acknowledging their gifts and graces (WLC Q. 144). By "covering over," the Divines certainly do not mean that we should provide cover for those who are involved in evil deeds, especially those who profess to be Christians. The ninth commandment requires us to confront evildoers and, in the case of crimes, to involve the civil magistrate (Eph. 5:11).

Rather, covering over our neighbor's infirmities means not airing their dirty laundry (for example, sharing embarrassing details of their former life of sin) and when we are offended by them, resisting the temptation to find a sympathetic ear and say, "Can you believe what so and so just said to me?" There is a place for letting our neighbor's words "roll off our back." Part of sanctification is developing thicker skin and a softer heart. The more sanctified we become the less we take offense and the more inclined we are to forgive.

Put On Truth
The first order of business in taming our fiery tongues (James 3:6) is to open our ears. James 1:19-20 says, "Know this, my beloved brothers: let every person be quick to hear, slow to speak, slow to anger; for the anger of man does not produce the righteousness of God." How many times have we secretly harbored anger and bitterness with a brother or sister in Christ, only to have that anger dissipate once we stopped to listen to their side of the story? We murdered them in our hearts based on a narrative that proved not to be true. Much of our sinful speech would be headed off at the pass if we stopped to listen and gain understanding. Being good speakers requires us to become good listeners.

Speaking the truth is one thing, but "speaking the truth in love" is quite another (Eph. 4:15). The saying, "You can catch more flies with honey than with vinegar" may not be scriptural, but it does echo Paul's exhortation in Galatians 6:1: "Brothers, if anyone is caught in any transgression, you who are spiritual should restore him in a *spirit of gentleness*" (emphasis added). What brother will be restored by being berated and belittled? No amount of failure on our brother's part entitles us to be acerbic in our speech; such speaking only adds further fuel to the fire and heaps shame upon our brother. Instead, we should be gracious and patient with our neighbor's failings and be careful not to break the bruised reeds or snuff out the faintly burning wicks among us (Isa. 42:3).

The ninth commandment also requires courage to speak the truth even when it is costly and unpopular. There are some things, no matter how conscientiously you say them, that will provoke unregenerate men (and even some professing believers) to anger. Previously vanilla statements like, "Marriage is between one man and one woman. Homosexuality is contrary to nature. There are only two genders." are now treated as hate speech in some parts of the world. What are Christians to do? We must be bold and courageous. We cannot remain silent. To hide the truth of God's Word from man is sin. If there is no other name under heaven by which men are saved, then it is imperative that we lift high the name of Jesus Christ and call on men to repent and believe in the gospel. Our God is a God of truth, and so we, His people, are to speak the truth in love our fellow man.

The Tenth Commandment

> *You shall not covet ...*
> —Exodus 20:17

When I first became a pastor, a ministry friend said to me, "Comparison is the thief of joy." Those words have stuck with me. Comparison is like the sun and discontentment a weed;

take away the one and you kill the other. Fundamental to our discontentment is the sin of pride. We consider ourselves more important than our neighbor and so naturally we believe that we deserve more possessions, more prominence, and a more satisfying life than him. We're not all that different from those laborers in the vineyard who begrudged their master's generosity shown to the laborers that were hired at the eleventh hour (Matt. 20:1-16) or the elder brother in the parable of the prodigal son (Luke 15:11-32). We say within our hearts, "Look at how hard I've worked! I've done all the right things. They don't deserve x, y, or z, but *I* do." What is this but a subtle form of works righteousness, of thinking that God becomes our debtor when we do what is right? Of course, such appeals to our worthiness fail to grasp the weight of what we really deserve (God's wrath and curse both in this life and that which is to come), but also the fact that, even if we did obey God's law perfectly, we would still only be doing our duty. We cannot go above and beyond the demands of God's law. We are all unprofitable servants (Luke 17:10), undeserving of even the least of His blessings. All that we are and all that we have is a consequence of His grace.

More Is Not Always More
When John D. Rockefeller was asked "How much money is enough?" the world's first billionaire replied, "Just a little bit more!" Never mind the fact that Rockefeller had more money than anyone else in the world at the time, Rockefeller needed just a little more to be satisfied. Such is the attitude of a discontented heart. Like a black hole that isn't satisfied even after consuming an entire planet, neither is the unregenerate heart satisfied even when it has virtually limitless earthly pleasures at its disposal.

King Solomon, an extravagantly wealthy man himself, saw things quite differently than the twentieth-century oil tycoon. Solomon recounts:

> So I became great and surpassed all who were before me in Jerusalem. Also my wisdom remained with me. And whatever my eyes desired I did not keep from them. I kept my heart from no pleasure, for my heart found pleasure in all my toil, and this was my reward for all my toil. Then I considered all that my hands had done and the toil I had expended in doing it, and behold, all was vanity and a striving after wind, and there was nothing to be gained under the sun. (Eccles. 2:9-11)

With his Spirit-guided wisdom intact, Solomon realized that the things of this world, no matter how much of them he acquired, could not satisfy the deepest longings of his soul. Earth's joys are vain and breathy, like a vapor in the wind, here one moment and gone the next. True and lasting contentment cannot be found in things that pass away. Rockefeller's answer, "Just a little bit more [vanity]" is a recipe for further discontentment and dissatisfaction. The answer for life's vanity is not "More vanity!"

For the Christian, true and lasting contentment is found in knowing Jesus Christ who is the same yesterday, today, and forever (Heb. 13:8), whose love is from everlasting to everlasting (Ps. 103:17), and who has purchased an inheritance for us that is imperishable, undefiled, unfading, and kept safe in heaven for us (1 Pet. 1:4). The reason that Christians can "give thanks in all circumstances" (1 Thess. 5:18) is because they always have Christ. True contentment is found only and always in Him.

3

The First Use

The Law as Mirror

In the days before photoshop and airbrushing, portrait painters were known for being *very* charitable to their human subjects. The standard practice was for the painter to leave out the wrinkles, blemishes, and bags under the model's eyes and to present an idealized version of the person sitting in front of them. One portrait that did not conform to this typical pattern was Sir Peter Lely's portrait of Oliver Cromwell, Lord Protector of the Commonwealth of England. In Lely's painting, Cromwell's visage is not at all flattering; his face is pocked with scars, warts, and the weathering of old age. So startlingly accurate was Lely's depiction of Cromwell that it gave rise to the legend that when Cromwell first sat for his portrait, he told Lely, "Paint me as I am, warts and all!"[1]

---

1 I am aware that this quotation was attributed to Cromwell approximately 100 years after his death and that it is unlikely that he used these exact words. However, the illustration holds in so far as Cromwell's portrait was an *accurate* depiction of his appearance and not an idealized version.

Sinful man, like a seventeenth-century portrait painter, loves to brush over his glaring defects and sin. The Moral Law, however, extends no such charity. It shows sinful man his true spiritual condition, warts and all. This is the first use of the Moral Law—it reveals who we really are and how desperately we need a Savior. Calvin likened this first use of the law to seeing oneself in a mirror: "Thus the Law is a kind of mirror. As in a mirror we discover any stains upon our face, so in the Law we behold, first, our impotence; then, in consequence of it, our iniquity; and, finally, the curse, as the consequence of both."[2] The law serves to show us our powerlessness to keep it and our condemnation for having broken it. But, praise God that it not only reveals our guilt but Him who is "the end of the law for righteousness to everyone who believes" (Rom. 10:4).

The first portion of this chapter will explore three basic ways that sinful man makes allowances for his sin and how the Moral Law leaves him without excuse (Rom. 1:20). The second portion will focus on Jesus Christ and how the law was designed to drive sinners to Him alone for the righteousness that God requires.

The Law Shows Us Our True Selves
Minimization
Whenever an elected official is at the center of a public scandal, whether it be misusing taxpayer dollars, an affair with a campaign staffer, or driving under the influence of drugs or alcohol, the language of damage control is never far away. "It was a momentary lapse in judgment … My opponents are making a mountain out of a mole hill … Nobody is perfect, everyone makes mistakes." But it is not just career politicians who minimize the seriousness of their wrongdoing using euphemism and spin—all of us have a knack for justifying our

2 Calvin, *Institutes*, 2.7.7.

sin. "I'm not overly critical, I'm just a perfectionist! I really want the team to succeed and it aggravates me when they underperform. I can't help that I have high standards," we explain. Or, "It was only a little white lie. I didn't want to hurt his feelings by telling the truth. Can you imagine how he would have responded if I told him what really happened?" These examples represent the lengths to which we will go to cushion the blow that comes with seeing, confessing, and repenting of our sin. This is the first hurdle that we must clear for repentance toward God to be genuine—we must have "a true sense of our sin" (WSC Q. 87). The only way that we will attain this true sense of sin is by seeing it from God's perspective—a perspective that has been revealed in the Ten Commandments.

As Paul notes from personal experience, the Moral Law exposes the true, soul-periling nature of sin to our minds. As the Westminster Confession says, "there is no sin so small, but it deserves damnation…" (WCF 15:4). All sin, however minute, is mortal. To convince us that this is so, God, in His mercy, gave the Moral Law to reveal the true weight of sin and the true costliness of Christ's sacrifice to redeem sinners. Seeing sin in actual size is the first step to "apprehending the mercy of God in Christ" (WSC Q. 87). The greater our sense of sin, the greater our appreciation for the breadth and depth of Christ's love for us.

In Romans 7, Paul says that the law showed him that he was dead where he once thought himself "alive," that he was guilty where he once thought himself blameless and without fault:

> Yet if it had not been for the law, I would not have known sin. For I would not have known what it is to covet if the law had not said, "You shall not covet." But sin, seizing an opportunity through the commandment, produced in me all kinds of covetousness. For apart from the law, sin lies dead. I was once

alive apart from the law, but when the commandment came, sin came alive and I died. (Rom. 7:7-9)

A few words of clarification. By "I would not have known sin" and "sin lies dead," Paul does not mean that he was free and innocent of all covetousness prior to knowing the tenth commandment in its written, Mosaic form. Paul says earlier in Romans that whether a person sins "without the law" (Gentiles) or "under the law" (Jews), "all have sinned and fall short of the glory of God" (Rom. 3:23). A person does not have to know they are sinning to be guilty of sin any more than a driver needs to know he was driving 100mph in a school zone to be given a hefty speeding ticket. "I'm sorry officer. I had no idea how fast I was going" doesn't change the speedometer one digit. Sinning against knowledge and sinning without knowledge are both still sin. What Paul means was that he did not fully grasp what covetousness was. To his mind covetousness lay dead—it wasn't on his radar. His lack of awareness begat a lack of conviction. But when, through the regenerating work of the Holy Spirit, Paul understood all that the tenth commandment required, only then did he realize that sin wasn't dead but that *he* was (Eph. 2:1). Like the rich young ruler before him who believed that he had kept God's law perfectly ever since his youth, God used the Moral Law in Paul's life to expose his covetousness and to convince him that he lacked the perfect righteousness that God required (Matt. 19:20).

And lest someone find fault with the law as though it had killed Paul (v. 10) or enticed him to sin, Paul stresses that it was not the law itself but his own corruption that was to blame: "*But sin*, seizing an opportunity through the commandment produced in me all kinds of covetousness" (v. 8, emphasis added). He continues in verse 13, "Did that which is good, then, bring death to me? By no means! *It was sin*, producing death in me through what is good ..." (emphasis added). Once he realized that he wasn't supposed to covet, his sinful heart coveted more and more. Paul's experience is akin to that of the parent who tells their child, "No cookies before dinner." only to find that the child is more determined to steal cookies from the cookie jar than before. The fault lies not with the law, but with the law-breaker: "The law is holy, and the commandment is holy and righteous and good" (v. 12). Paul understood that the abuse of a good thing doesn't make a good thing bad.[3] Because the desires of Paul's heart were not right within him, the law had a deadening effect upon him.

The nineteenth-century Episcopalian, Stephen Tyng, writes that the Moral Law, besides convincing us of sin's enormity, also convinces us that we are guilty of a greater number of sins than we previously imagined:

> Under this operation of the law, man becomes consciously condemned, and without hope. The law has brought to him a knowledge of his sin, and made his offenses to abound in his view. And under this reviving power of sin which it brings to light, he dies to all prospect or means of finding acceptance with God in any character of his own.[4]

This making sin to "abound" in our view is what Paul has in mind in Romans 5. After speaking of Christ's obedience being the means whereby many will be made righteous (v. 19), Paul

---

3 Anthony Burgess wrote, "It is true that misusing the Law, not as God intended, can harm and poison us, much like when the Manna was kept improperly and turned into worms" (*Vindiciae Legis: A Vinidication of the Moral Law and the Covenants,* [West Linn, OR: Monergism Books, 2023], 18). Like the law, the manna was a good gift from God, but because the people stubbornly refused to use the manna in the way that God had prescribed, it became harmful and odious to them.

4 Stephen Tyng, *Lectures on the Law & the Gospel* (Birmingham, AL: Solid Ground Christian Books, 2008), 72.

anticipates the question, "Then what was the purpose of the law? If God did not give it for the purpose of earning eternal life, then why did He give it at all?" He responds, "Now the law came in to increase the trespass, but where sin increased, grace abounded all the more" (Rom. 5:20). By "increase" Paul means increasing our sense of sin's extent, not the frequency with which we commit sin. As John Newton said so well, "The law entered, that sin might abound: not to make men more wicked, though occasionally and by abuse it has that effect, but to make them sensible how wicked they are."[5] We see sin in places that we hadn't seen it before. In this way the law acts like a magnifying glass that, as Matthew Henry says, "discovers the spots, but does not cause them. When the commandment came into the world sins revived, as the letting of a clear light into a room discovers the dust and filth which were there before, but were not seen."[6] The law discovers sin but never causes it. Like a light that shines into a dark and dusty room, so too do we need the light of God's law to shine into our hearts that we might discern our errors and be cleansed of our hidden faults (Ps. 19:12). The law, rightly used, convinces us that our sin is greater in size and greater in number than we ever could have imagined.

Comparison

Besides minimization, sinful man excuses his sin by comparing his conduct with that of his neighbor, especially that neighbor who is guilty of some scandalous sin. The lower we set the bar, the better we feel by comparison. Like the Pharisee in the temple, we are quick to find the tax collector nearest us and exclaim within our hearts, "God, I thank you that I am not like other men, extortioners, unjust, adulterers, or even this tax

---

5 John Newton, *The Works of John Newton,* vol.1, 246.

6 Matthew Henry, *Matthew Henry's Commentary on the Whole Bible,* (Peabody, MA: Hendrickson Publishers, 1991), 2206.

collector" (Luke 18:11). Our chests swell with pride that we aren't as bad as *that* person.

The Moral Law shatters such notions of self-righteousness. In Romans 2, Paul confronts members of the Jewish community who felt morally superior to the Gentiles who were guilty of the sins listed in Romans 1. One can almost hear the proud Jewish reader breathe a sigh of relief, saying, "Whew, glad I'm not filled with all manner of unrighteousness, evil, covetousness, malice, envy, murder, strife, deceit, and maliciousness (Rom. 1:29). I can't wait for those Gentiles to suffer the judgment of God stored up for them!" Paul says "Not so fast!" He argues that the Jews were in no position to stand in judgment over their neighbors because they practiced the very same things (v. 1). They preached against stealing and yet they stole. They said one must not commit adultery while they committed adultery themselves (vv. 22-23). They fancied themselves as guides to the blind, but in reality they were blind themselves, groping about in moral darkness (v. 19). They were hypocrites of the first order. In fact, the Jews were actually *more* guilty than the Gentiles because the Jews sinned against knowledge and against the riches of God's kindness and forbearance and patience (v. 4). The Jews had the law, they had circumcision, they had the oracles of God, they of all people should have known better, but their reception of the law did not cause them to live any better than the Gentiles they so despised. Because their hearts were "hard and impenitent," that which should have caused them to beat their chests in humility, to cry out to God for mercy, and to look on their fellow man with sympathy and compassion, actually became the means of storing up wrath for themselves at the day of Christ's coming (v. 5).

In Romans 2:13, Paul corrects the Jewish misconception that their reception of the Moral Law automatically made or confirmed them as righteous: "For it is not the hearers of the law who are righteous before God, but the doers of the law who will be justified." Paul's point is that if one wants to be justified by the Moral Law, the mere hearing of it will do them no good; the only way to be made righteous via the law is to keep it personally, perfectly, and perpetually. And, seeing that no one, whether Jew or Gentile, ever has, Paul is redirecting his reader's attention away from obedience to the Moral Law as the means of attaining eternal life, and to faith in Him who has satisfied the demands of the law and gives His righteousness to sinners as a gift.

God's revealing the Moral Law to Israel was a unique, covenantal privilege. No other nation had the Ten Commandments delivered to them in written form from God's own hand (Rom. 3:1). And yet, receiving and hearing the law did not save a single Israelite. They, like the rest of humanity, were cut from the same sinful bolt of cloth. As Paul says, "What then? Are we Jews any better off?" Are they more naturally righteous than the Gentiles as they suppose? "No, not at all. For we have already charged that all, both Jews and Greeks, are under sin, as it is written: 'None is righteous, no, not one; no one understands; no one seeks for God" (Rom. 3:9-11). All men are guilty and stand in need of a righteousness that comes from without and not within.

On the Last Day when Christ comes and all are raised to stand before the great white throne of judgment, He will not be grading on a curve. The standard will not be "Were you better than this person or that person? Did you do more good deeds and fewer evil deeds than them?" The point of comparison will not be our neighbor but the Moral Law and whether we have perfectly obeyed its commands in the inner and outer man— "He will render to each one according to his works" (Rom. 2:6). Of course, none of us have kept God's law perfectly, "For all who rely on works of the law are under a curse; for it is written,

'Cursed be everyone who does not abide by all things written in the Book of the Law, and do them'" (Gal. 3:10). But that is precisely the reason for which Christ came, to redeem "us from the curse of the law by becoming a curse for us" (Gal. 3:13). We will stand either upon our own merits or Christ's merits in the day of judgment. Either we will bear the curse due to us for sin or Christ will have borne the curse for us through His death in our place. The choice is easy, if only we judge ourselves according to the right standard.

Blame Shifting

Blame shifting is at the root of every half-hearted apology. We see it in the husband who justifies his adulterous affair saying, "I'm sorry for what I did, but you've been cold and distant lately. What choice did I have?" Or in the employee who is caught stealing from his employer, "I know I shouldn't have taken the money, but you left me no choice. I've been overworked and underpaid for far too long. I needed to provide for my family somehow." But blame shifting doesn't always need an individual to serve as the scapegoat. Difficult circumstances can also provide the cover we need: "Look, I know I lost my temper with you and the kids, but work has just been so stressful lately. If only you understood the pressure that I'm under, then you wouldn't be so hard on me." Notice the word "but" and how in each example it transforms what should be a sincere apology into veiled finger pointing—"I wouldn't have done this, if you hadn't done that." Instead of bringing two estranged parties together, blame shifting acts like a wedge driving them further and further apart.

This tactic traces its roots all the way back to the Garden of Eden. When God asked Adam whether he had eaten the forbidden fruit, Adam blame shifted, saying, "The woman that you gave to be with me, she gave me the fruit of the tree, and

I ate" (Gen. 3:12). Not only did Adam throw his wife under the bus for his disobedience, but he groused at God for giving him such a lousy temptress for a wife! It was everyone's fault but his own—that was Adam's thinking. Though Eve did sin in believing the lying serpent instead of the one true God, as my ethics professor in seminary used to quip, "You never have a right to do wrong." Wrong as she was, Adam could not blame Eve for his decision to violate God's command to not eat of the tree. The decision to eat was his own and so was the blame.

We see blame shifting elsewhere in the Old Testament, most notably in Ezekiel 18 when God confronts those who were bemoaning that they were still in exile in Babylon: "The word of the Lord came to me: 'What do you mean by repeating this proverb concerning the land of Israel, "The fathers have eaten sour grapes, and the children's teeth are set on edge"? As I live, declares the Lord God, this proverb shall no more be used by you in Israel'" (Ezek. 18:1-3).

One can hear the exiles' resentment toward God in the biting words of the proverb. The exiles, by and large, believed that God was unjustly punishing them for sins they had not committed (vv. 25, 29). It was their fathers' sin that prompted the Babylonian exile, not theirs, and yet here they were, left to die outside of the Promised Land.

But God refused to let their excuses stand. The reason Israel remained in exile was not because they were suffering for someone else's sins. The exiles were suffering for their own sin. In answer to their proverb God offers a proverb of His own:

> Behold, all souls are mine; the soul of the father as well as the soul of the son is mine: the soul that sins shall die…The soul that sins shall die. The son shall not suffer for the iniquity of the father, nor the father suffer for the iniquity of the son. The righteousness of the righteous shall be upon himself, and the wickedness of the wicked shall be upon himself. (vv. 4, 20)

God declares that He is perfectly just in all His dealings with man. The one who dies for sin dies for sins that *he* has committed. Even if his earthly father was guilty of awful sin, God's promise is that if and when a man "walks in my statutes, and keeps my rules by acting faithfully—he is righteous; he shall surely live, declares the Lord God" (v. 9). Every man will be held accountable for his own sin and not for the sins of any other.

Though there are places in Scripture, like the second commandment, where God says that He will visit "the iniquity of the fathers on the children to the third and fourth generation of those who hate me" (Exod. 20:5) such visitations are not punitive in nature. Matthew Henry writes:

> It is only in temporal calamities that children (and sometimes innocent ones) fare the worse for their parents' wickedness, and God can alter the property of those calamities, and make them work for good to those that are visited with them; but as to spiritual and eternal misery (and that is the death here spoken of) the children shall by no means smart for the parents' sins.[7]

In other words, God's warning is that the negative impacts ("temporal calamities") of sin, not sin's guilt, will extend to the children of those who continue in unrepentant sin. Sadly, we see this happen all the time. The child of a substance abuser grows up to be a substance abuser himself. Children whose parents were in and out of jail are far more likely to be in trouble with the law when they reach adulthood. This is a lamentable reality and one to which God's people should respond with mercy, compassion, and the hope of the gospel. God's amazing grace breaks even generational cycles of sin! Sympathetic as we should be, however, Scripture is clear that upon Jesus' return, all mankind will be judged impartially and "according to each

---

7 Henry, *Commentary,* 1374.

one's deeds" (1 Pet. 1:17). Apart from Adam's original guilt, no one ever has been or can be condemned or absolved upon the basis of someone else's sin, but praise be to God that all those who ever have been or will be saved are saved through the righteousness of another, namely Jesus Christ!

In the New Testament, Paul addresses blame shifting as it relates to God's sovereign decree of election and reprobation. In response to the word that God has mercy on whomever He wills and that He hardens whomever He wills, Paul anticipates the objection, "You will say to me then, 'Why does he still find fault? For who can resist his will?'" (Rom. 9:19). Paul's answer, "But who are you, O man, to answer back to God? Will what is molded say to its molder, 'Why have you made me like this?' Has the potter no right over the clay, to make out of the same lump one vessel for honorable use and another for dishonorable use?" (Rom. 9:20). While Paul's answer may not resolve every difficulty about the relationship between human responsibility and divine sovereignty, it does make clear that we cannot blame God for our sin. God is within His rights as the Creator to make some men, like Pharaoh (Rom. 9:17), as vessels to show forth His almighty power and justice and to make others for the display of His mercy and grace.

Before shifting gears from blame shifting, consider this— whenever we sin it is because we've freely chosen to do so. There is no circumstance in life wherein we can legitimately say, "I had no choice. I was forced to sin so I cannot be blamed." Paul tells us that this is never the case in 1 Corinthians 10:13: "No temptation has overtaken you that is not common to man. God is faithful, and he will not let you be tempted beyond your ability, but with the temptation he will also provide the way of escape, that you may be able to endure it." If God always provides a way of escape, then sin is never our only option. God never promised that obedience would be the easiest or most expedient option. It may cost us our reputation, our money, or even our lives. Obedience requires us to deny ourselves, to take up our crosses, and to follow Jesus even as our Lord obeyed His Father to the point of death, even death upon a cross (Luke 9:23; Phil. 2:8). God's promise is that whenever we are tempted, He will always present us with an obedient means of escape. It is our responsibility to avail ourselves of that escape and when we don't, the blame is ours alone.

Jesus' sinless life is the ultimate confirmation of what Paul is saying in 1 Corinthians 10:13. Because Christ was tried to a degree that no human being ever has been or will be, and yet was without sin, the argument that there are some situations in *our* lives so tempting that there is no choice but to sin falls utterly flat. If Christ was under no external necessity to sin when faced with greater temptation, then we are certainly under no external necessity to sin when faced with lesser temptations. As the writer of Hebrews says, "Consider him who endured from sinners such hostility against himself, so that you may not grow weary or fainthearted. In your struggle against sin you have not yet resisted to the point of shedding your blood" (Heb. 12:3-4). Whether in the wilderness with Satan, in the Garden of Gethsemane, or the cross whereupon He died, Jesus' thoughts, words, and deeds were in perfect conformity to the Moral Law.

Of course, there is a noteworthy difference between us and Christ—He was sinless (impeccable) and we are not. Christ was, as Thomas Boston once said, *non posse peccare* (not able to sin), by virtue of the union of His human nature with His divine nature. Nevertheless, Christ's impeccability does not undermine Paul's point. It establishes it. The problem, at its root, is a problem of nature, not circumstance. Christ did not sin because His nature was perfect; we sin because our nature is imperfect and blameworthy. It will not suffice for us to throw up our hands and say with the blame shifter in James 1, "I am being tempted by God" as though His providence were to blame for our sin. No, James is right in saying, "each person is tempted when he is lured and enticed by his own desire" (James 1:14). The root of our sin problem always lies within.

The Law Drives Us to Christ for Grace
Christ the Great Physician (Mark 2:17)
With such a bleak description of man's fallen condition, one may question whether there is any hope for guilty sinners. The good news of the gospel, however, is that there is abundant hope in Christ Jesus (Rom. 7:25a) for all who see their inward defilement and come to Christ for cleansing. Calvin, after laying his reader low, with a tender pastor's heart takes the humbled sinner by the hand and leads him to a willing Christ who hushed the law's loud thunder and quenched Mt. Sinai's flame through His satisfaction of all the law's demands.[8]

> But while the unrighteousness and condemnation of all are attested by the Law, it does not follow (if we make the proper use of it) that we are immediately to give up all hope and rush headlong on despair. No doubt, it has some such effect upon the reprobate, but this is owing to their obstinacy. With the children of God the effect is different…that feeling how naked and destitute they are, they may take refuge in His mercy, rely upon it, and cover themselves up entirely with it; renouncing all righteousness and merit, and clinging to mercy alone, as offered in Christ to all who long and look for it in true faith.[9]

Calvin goes on to quote Augustine who said of this use of the law, "The utility of the law is, that it convinces man of his

---

8 From the hymn "Let Us Love and Sing and Wonder" by John Newton.

9 Calvin, *Institutes*, 2.7.8.

weakness, and compels him to apply for the medicine of grace, which is in Christ."[10]

I for one hate going to see the doctor. Part of it, I am sure, is due to my upbringing (I promise I'm not blame shifting). For context, I come from a home where if you suffered from a high fever, a pounding headache, or severed a limb, Ibuprofen was considered the cure-all. "Give it fifteen minutes and you'll be fine."

The deeper reason why I hate going to the doctor is because I have a tendency to fear the worst. "Sir, I'm sorry to tell you this, but you have cancer"—who wants to hear those words? Certainly not me! So what is my solution? I avoid the doctor. I put off that check up another month, and then another month, and before long it has been years since I've seen a doctor. "Ignorance is bliss" is not the way to steward our mortal bodies. It is, however, the way that many steward their immortal souls. They avoid examining themselves by the Moral Law because they *know*, whether they will admit it or not, that their diagnosis is dire and that they cannot save themselves.

The first use of the law is a blessing to a sinner in the same way that a right diagnosis from a medical doctor is a blessing to a sick patient. If the patient never receives a proper diagnosis of what ails him, or worse, if he is lied to and given a clean bill of health (Jer. 6:14; 8:11), then he will never avail himself of the remedies that would heal him. The law, like an x-ray, exposes secret, hidden sins that if left untreated will fester and consume us. Self-medicating will not do. The law drives us outside of ourselves to the only one who can heal us, to Jesus Christ the Great Physician of our souls. Yes, our diagnosis is grim, but the grace and power of Christ that caused the blind to see, the lame to leap like a deer, and the tongue of the mute to sing for joy

---

10 ibid., 2.7.9.

(Isa. 35:5, 6) is able to take the sinner, dead in trespasses and sins, and raise him to newness of life (Rom. 6:4).

This spiritual newness of life was the purpose of Christ's miraculous physical healings. They were visible means of communicating a deeper spiritual message. When Jesus healed the paralytic who was lowered through the roof, His first words were not about the man's physical condition but his spiritual condition: "Son, your sins are forgiven" (Mark 2:5). Problematic as the man's paralysis was, Jesus knew that his sinful heart was the most pressing issue. And when He finally did heal the paralytic, *why* did Jesus heal him? "'But that you may know that the Son of Man has authority on earth to forgive sins'—he said to the paralytic—'I say to you, rise, pick up your bed, and go home'" (Mark 2:10-11). The healing was a demonstration of Christ's divine power, yes, but even more importantly that Christ, as God, is willing and able to forgive sin. Have you received the Moral Law's diagnosis? Have you allowed it to search you, to sift you, and reveal your hidden faults? If so, the gospel calls you not to despair but to flee to Christ Jesus. Waste no more time and come to the Great Physician who delights in healing the broken-hearted and binding up their wounds (Ps. 147:3).

Christ the End of the Law (Romans 10:4)
What does it mean that Christ is the end of the law? Some infer from these words that Christ brings an end to the demands of the Mosaic Law. "We are no longer under the Old Covenant rites and ceremonies," they will say. In that sense, they are correct. The Ceremonial and Civil Laws have been fulfilled by Christ and believers are no longer obligated, nay, they are *commanded* to not turn back to the shadowy forms of the Old Covenant as it would amount to a rejection of Christ's finished work upon the cross (Gal. 5:1-6; Heb. 10:1-4). But in

the context of Romans 10, Paul has the Moral Law particularly in view. So in what sense is Christ the end of the Moral Law?

At one level, Scripture teaches that believers have been freed from obedience to the Moral Law *as the means of attaining justifying righteousness.* As John Colquhoun writes, "The law as a covenant is dead to believers since it will not and cannot exercise any commanding or condemning power over them. It can neither justify them for their personal obedience nor condemn them for their disobedience."[11] Calvin likewise speaks of the Moral Law being abrogated in the sense that the law "is not to believers what it formerly was; in other words, that it does not, by terrifying and confounding their consciences, condemn and destroy. It is certainly true that Paul shows, in clear terms, that there is such an abrogation of the Law."[12] God's people are no longer under the bondage and condemnation of the Covenant of Works as they were before their conversion. The law's legal, punitive claims upon them have ended, but not its guiding and governing power as we will see in the final chapter.[13]

The second way that "end" is used, and the way that Paul is using it in Romans 10, refers to Christ as the goal of the Moral Law.[14] He is the law's realization, its *telos,* fulfillment,

---

11 Colquhoun, *The Law and the Gospel,* 175.

12 Calvin, *Institutes,* 2.7.14.

13 Samuel Bolton writes in *The True Bounds of Christian Freedom* (Edinburgh: Banner of Truth, 2020, 32-33) that the Christian, "is not under it [the Moral Law] as a court. He is not under the law as a covenant of life and death. As he is in Christ, he is under the covenant of grace…He is under its guidance, not under its curses, under its precepts (though not on the legal condition of 'Do this and live'), but not under its penalties…It may condemn sin in us, but cannot condemn us for sin". Also, Anthony Burgess writes, "Although the Law does not curse or condemn the believer in terms of their state, it does condemn the particular sins they commit, which are guilty of God's wrath. However, this guilt does not extend to the person" (*Vindiciae Legis,* 16).

14 See Ernest Kevan, *The Moral Law,* 109.

perfection, Accomplisher, Satisfier, and Keeper. He is the sum and substance of the righteousness and holiness of which the Moral Law is the shadow.

If we take a step back, the relationship between Christ and the law bears resemblance to Christ's relationship to the sacraments. The Reformed tradition has always maintained that baptism and the Lord's Supper, in and of themselves, do not have the power to save (WCF 27:2). They are signs, not the things they signify. They are not ends in themselves but means to the end of Christ whose person and work they picture. So it is with the law. Christ is the end and the law is His means of hastening sinners on to Him for their salvation. Ever since Adam's fall, this has always been the case. The law was never laid down to save, as Stephen Tyng reminds us: "It was not designed to open a way of safety and life to transgressors in their own obedience. Its purpose was directly the reverse. It invited none. It faithfully and solemnly warned all, to fly from its sentence, and from the attempt to gain acceptance by fulfilling it."[15]

Any attempt to use the Moral Law for justification represents a fundamental misunderstanding of the purpose for which God revealed it. We were never meant to turn to the law in the hope of being our own saviors.[16] When He revealed the Moral Law at Mt. Sinai, God was not establishing a new Covenant of Works. Had He been, it would have nullified the promise that God made to Abraham in Genesis 15, which is impossible—God always keeps His promises! This is the crux of Paul's argument in Galatians 3—the coming of the Moral

---

15 Tyng, *Lectures on the Law & the Gospel,* 115. In this same vein, Samuel Bolton writes, "The law shows us what is good, but gives us no power to do it ... The law shows us what is holy, but cannot make us holy, as long as it is a rule outside of us. It cannot make us holy, for that necessitates a rule within us" (*True Bounds of Christian Freedom,* 87).

16 Burgess, *Vindiciae Legis,* 23.

Law 430 years after the promises made to Abraham proves that it was not given as a means of securing eternal life but that it has always been subservient to the purposes of the Gospel.[17]

> This is what I mean: the law, which came 430 years afterward, does not annul a covenant previously ratified by God, so as to make the promise void. For if the inheritance comes by the law, it no longer comes by promise; but God gave it to Abraham by a promise. Why then the law? *It was added because of transgressions…*Is the law then contrary to the promises of God? Certainly not! For if a law had been given that could give life, then righteousness would indeed be by the law (Gal. 3:17-19a, 21, emphasis added).

Paul's answer to "Why then the law?" is not "for justification." It is, "because of transgressions." This echoes Romans 3:20 ("since through the law comes knowledge of sin") and Romans 5:20 ("Now the law came in to increase the trespass")—the law was given to *teach,* not to save![18] If the law could save then Christ died for no purpose (Gal. 2:21). The shedding of Christ's blood would have been superfluous if all that salvation required was more effort on our part.

Relying upon works of the law instead of Christ's work only brings weariness and despair upon the worker. The law "acts as an hard task-master, requiring us to make brick, and furnishing us with no straw."[19] Samuel Bolton argued that

---

17 Samuel Bolton, "There was no end or use for which the law was originally given but is consistent with grace, and serviceable to the advancement of the covenant of grace," (*The True Bounds of Christian Freedom*, 59).

18 Tyng, "It has justification for none. The purpose of its convincing operation is to exhibit distinctly this fact. And when it has brought the sinner to this despair in himself, by shewing him his unspeakable dangers, and his inability to find a remedy for them, by any thing he can do or suffer, it has finished its work," (*Lectures on the Law & the Gospel*, 75).

19 ibid., 132, 75.

every effort to merit salvation, far from alleviating our misery, actually compounds and deepens it:

> We were not able to weep, to pray, to work ourselves out of this condition. It is with us as with men caught in quicksands; the more they strive, the deeper they sink into them. So the more we strive in our own strength and by our own power, the more we become entangled, and the stronger the chain becomes which binds us to this condition.[20]

What a fitting description of the experience of the Protestant Reformer, Martin Luther. Despite the countless hours spent in confession, beating himself with whips, starving himself through many fasts, and shedding rivers of tears, Luther was never able to shake that sinking feeling that he was beneath God's righteous frown. No amount of works, however costly, were able to soothe his guilty conscience. But when he trusted in Christ alone for his justification, his life was forever changed. Perhaps you feel a Luther-like burden yourself. You walk on spiritual eggshells constantly, always fearful that you will fall out of favor with God if you fall back into that besetting sin. If so, remember Christ's call to those who are bowed down and weary with their sin and strivings, "Come to me, all who labor and are heavy laden, and I will give you rest. Take my yoke upon you, and learn from me, for I am gentle and lowly in heart, and you will find rest for your souls. For my yoke is easy, and my burden is light" (Matt. 11:28-30). You cannot work yourself out of your sinful condition. There is nothing lacking in Christ's wounds that you can supply by your own obedience. The words of the hymn "Rock of Ages, Cleft for Me" seem especially fitting here:

---

20 Bolton, *The True Bounds of Christian Freedom*, 214.

Not the labors of my hands
Can fulfill thy law's demands;
could my zeal no respite know,
Could my tears forever flow,
All for sin could not atone;
thou must save, and thou alone.

Nothing in my hands I bring,
simply to thy cross I cling;
naked come to thee for dress;
Helpless look to thee for grace'
Foul, I to the fountain fly;
wash me, Savior, or I die. [21]

All you can do is come to Christ with the open hands of faith. There is no one beside Him, no one beyond Him, and so when you come to Christ you will find in Him all that you need. Fly to Him and receive true and lasting rest for your soul.

---

21 From the hymn "Rock of Ages, Cleft for Me" by Augustus Toplady.

4

The Second Use

The Law as Muzzle

In an article from the American Kennel Club titled, "Dog Muzzles: When, Why, and How to Correctly Use Them" certified professional dog trainer, Stephanie Gibeault, argues that there are several scenarios wherein it is good and humane to muzzle a dog. When a dog is injured and in distress it is highly probable that the dog will lash out and bite the person trying to help it. A muzzle offers protection for the caregiver and gets the dog the help it needs in a timely fashion. If a dog is nervous during a grooming session or feels threatened by another dog, a muzzle is a good way to protect all parties until the stressful situation has passed. If a dog has a history of aggression and has bitten other animals or people in the past, a muzzle ensures that nobody else will be attacked. "However," Gibeault writes, "the muzzle doesn't solve the problem, it simply helps keep everybody safe while you work on behavior modification with an animal behaviorist, veterinarian, and/or dog trainer. Your goal should be to change your dog's behavior and mindset. The muzzle is simply a temporary tool to help you achieve that goal."[1]

Gibeault's description of a muzzle's function for a dog parallels nicely with the second use of the Moral Law for man. Here are her words (slightly) edited for the purposes of this chapter: "The muzzle *(Moral Law)* doesn't solve the problem, it simply helps keep everybody safe while you work on *the sinner's heart through the preaching of the Word, the administration of the sacraments, prayer, and all in dependence upon the Holy Spirit.* Your goal should be *your neighbor's conversion,* a change *of heart and mind.* The muzzle *(Moral Law)* is simply a temporary tool to help you achieve that goal."

This chapter will first explain how the Moral Law restrains human sinfulness internally via fear and the positive impact that this restraint has upon society as a whole. Then, it will address the question with which Christians have wrestled throughout the ages, especially: to what extent is the civil magistrate responsible to curb evil? Asked another way, should believers expect the state to punish violations of the first *and* second tables of the law? I don't expect to resolve every difficulty surrounding this question; however I hope to provide a basic framework for every believer to identify the responsibilities belonging to the church and state, within their respective spheres, and how to be a faithful witness for Christ in all of life.

The Moral Law Restrains Wickedness Through Fear

Many of us have had an authority figure in our lives, whether it was our father or mother, a grandparent, a teacher, or a coach who "put the fear of God in us." Properly speaking, it wasn't

---

1 Stephanie Gibeault, "When, Why, and How to Correctly Use Dog Muzzles." *American Kennel Club.* June 3, 2024. Accessed May 27, 2024, https://www.akc.org/expert-advice/training/dog-muzzles-when-why-how-to-use/.

God that we grew to fear but the authority figure themselves. The Moral Law, on the other hand, actually puts the fear of God in us. Ideally this law-inspired fear (we pray) will result in genuine grief and sorrow for sin, repentance, and faith in Jesus Christ. The goal of Sinai's blazing fire, darkness, gloom, and tempest that made Moses say, "I tremble with fear," is to hasten us on to Mount Zion, to Jesus Christ the mediator of the New Covenant (Heb. 12:18-24). Nevertheless, even if it does not result in conversion, the Moral law produces an inward fear and dread of God's wrath that restrains the unbeliever's evil desires and keeps them from breaking forth into outward action.

Calvin writes of this restraining effect in the *Institutes:*

> The second office of the Law is, by means of its fearful denunciations and the consequent dread of punishment, to curb those who, unless forced, have no regard for rectitude and justice. Such persons are curbed not because their mind is inwardly moved and affected, but because, as if a bridle were laid upon them, they refrain their hands from external acts, and internally check the depravity which would otherwise petulantly burst forth.[2]

This is what Paul means in 1 Timothy 1:8-11. The law, rightly used, keeps the depravity of the unregenerate heart in check:

> Now we know that the law is good, if one uses it lawfully, understanding this, *that the law is not laid down for the just but for the lawless and disobedient*, for the ungodly and sinners, for the unholy and profane, for those who strike their fathers and mothers, for murderers, the sexually immoral, men who practice homosexuality, enslavers, liars, perjurers, and whatever else is contrary to sound doctrine, in accordance with the gospel of the glory of the blessed God with which I have been entrusted (Emphasis added).

---

2 Calvin, *Institutes*, 2.7.10.

Believing and Unbelieving Fear

When Paul says "that the law is not laid down for the just but for the lawless and disobedient," he is not suggesting that the law is altogether unprofitable to the just (i.e. believers, those who are declared just in and through Jesus Christ) or that there is no sense in which fear deters believers from sin. There is a godly, submissive fear that God's people are to have toward Him at all times. Consider Psalm 2:11 where service, fear, and joy are commanded side by side—"Serve the LORD with fear, and rejoice with trembling"—and Psalm 112:1 where the fear of God is presented as the key to a blessed life—"Praise the LORD! Blessed is the man who fears the LORD, who greatly delights in his commandments!"[3] And who can forget the words of Solomon: "The fear of the Lord is the beginning of wisdom, and the knowledge of the Holy One is insight" (Prov. 9:10)?

The sense of fear that believers have toward God is filial in nature, like that of a son who fears his father's chastening rod, not like a criminal who fears the judge's gavel. John Bunyan highlights this distinction in his treatise on the fear of God: "But I would not have them [believers] fear with the fear of slaves; for that will add no strength against sin; but I would have them fear with the reverential fear of sons; and that is the way to depart from the devil."[4] Upon his conversion, the believer's highest motivation for mortifying sin and pursuing obedience shifts from fear of God to love for God. Jesus said to His disciples, "If you love me, you will keep my commandments" (John 14:15).

---

3 See also Ps. 34:9, 11; Ps. 47:2; Ps 86:11; Ps 103:13; Ps. 111:10; Prov 19:23.

4 John Bunyan, *A Treatise on the Fear of God* (Edinburgh: The Banner of Truth Trust, 2018), 56. Samuel Bolton speaks of a twofold subjection to the law and how the believer's subjection is not contrary to, but is the very essence of Christian freedom, "We are freed from the one, namely the subjection of a slave, which was part of our bondage, but not from the other, namely the subjection of a son, which is part of our freedom" (*The True Bounds of Christian Freedom,* 40).

Fear is a true and necessary motivation for obedience in the Christian life, but love for Christ must always enjoy pride of place. The redeemed tread the paths of righteousness *willingly,* as sheep follow the voice of the shepherd whom they know and love (Ps. 23:3; John 10:27).

Paul's point is this—those whose hearts have been renewed by the Holy Spirit and who now delight in the law of God in their inmost being (Rom. 7:22), do not need the law to inspire an abject fear of suffering under God's eternal punishment to keep them from sinning anymore. Paul reminds the Romans that if they are in union with Christ through faith (and they were) then that makes them God's adopted children. They cannot be disinherited; they are forever secure and cannot and will not finally fall away (WCF 17:1). Consequently, they should not succumb to that *type* of fear any longer: "For you did not receive the spirit of slavery to fall back into fear, but you have received the Spirit of adoption as sons, by whom we cry, 'Abba! Father!'" (Rom. 8:15).

Think back to the muzzle analogy. A dog that has been properly trained by its master does not need a muzzle to keep it from biting others. That is not its way anymore. A muzzle is not *for* such a dog. So it is with the law—the law is laid down as a means of terrifying only those whose hearts have "no regard for rectitude or justice" as Calvin said. Their hearts are as hostile to God and contrary to holiness as ever.

The Hardening and Softening Effects of Fear

The instilling of fear and restraint will have one of two effects upon the unregenerate—they will either grow to hate God and His law with an even deeper hatred (Ps. 2:1-3), like a lion who is enraged after being muzzled and locked in a cage, or they will become (unbeknownst to them at the time) more acquainted with the manner of living that they will fully and joyfully embrace in the day of their conversion.

Listen to the way that Calvin describes these effects of fear:

> Nay, the more they restrain themselves, the more they are inflamed, the more they rage and boil, prepared for any act or outbreak whatsoever were it not for the terror of the law. And not only so, but they thoroughly detest the law itself, and execrate the Lawgiver; so that if they could they would most willingly annihilate Him, because they cannot bear either His ordering what is right, or His avenging of the despisers of His majesty...this tuition is not without its use, even to the children of God, who, previous to their effectual calling, being destitute of the Spirit of holiness, freely indulge the lusts of the flesh. When, by fear of Divine vengeance, they are deterred from open outbreaking, though, from not being subdued in mind, they profit little at present, still they are in some measure trained to bear the yoke of righteousness, so that when they are called, they are not like mere novices, studying a discipline of which previously they had no knowledge.[5]

Let this line sink in: "They are still in some measure trained to bear the yoke of righteousness." Some, upon hearing these words, may think that Calvin sounds like those men during the Puritan era who espoused what is called *preparationism*, the belief that a sinner must do something or feel a certain degree of grief or sorrow before answering the call of the gospel. Calvin's theology of conversion, however, is in perfect harmony with Westminster Confession 16:7: "Works done by unregenerate man, although for the matter of them they may be things which God commands...cannot please God, or make a man meet to receive grace from God." The "training" is not something that the sinner undergoes as a prerequisite for

---

5 Calvin, *Institutes,* 2.7.10

receiving grace, but, from the divine vantage point, it is God's means of preserving and preparing the sinner for the day of his salvation. Calvin writes later:

> Those, therefore, whom He has destined to the inheritance of His kingdom, if He does not immediately regenerate, He, through the works of the law, preserves in fear, against the time of His visitation, not, indeed, that pure and chaste fear which His children ought to have, but a fear useful to the extent of instructing them in true piety according to their capacity.[6]

We could say that God, through the ministry of the Spirit, mysteriously acquaints the not-yet-believer with a basic understanding of what righteousness is before he comes to know and possess it fully on the day when he looks to Christ in faith.

Those who grew up in Christian homes but were not converted until later in life are a textbook example of the person Calvin has in mind. Perhaps this is your experience. You memorized the Shorter Catechism (mostly), went to church every Sunday morning (and evening, too), and always did as you were told—you didn't smoke, chew, or run with those that do, and yet, underneath this external adherence to the Moral Law, you didn't trust in Christ until you were an adult. Were all those years a waste? By no means! Though you did not have "that pure and chaste fear which His children ought to have," God providentially placed you in a believing home and a local church to guard and shield you from the ruinous effects of those sins you would have committed had you not been kept in check by their restraining influence. And when you came to saving faith, the Christian lifestyle was not altogether foreign to you. Your transition from darkness to

---

6 Calvin, *Institutes*, 2.7.11

light was smoother than that of the serial adulterer, the violent criminal, or the substance abuser whose experience was like that of the teenager whose eyes are blinded when his parent suddenly throws open the shades of his pitch-black bedroom. Old habits die hard. And though the law cannot save before conversion, the fear it inspires can spare us from needless pain and misery.

John Newton's best-known hymn speaks to the importance of this fear in the experience of conversion:

> 'Twas grace that taught my heart to fear,
> and grace my fears relieved,
> how precious did that grace appear,
> the hour I first believed.[7]

Take a moment to consider all the sins that God has delivered and *kept* you from. Think of all that could have happened to you if God had let you go altogether. And think of all that He has brought you to. He loved you and kept you, long before you ever knew Him. Oh how patient and gracious God is to His sheep even as they wander!

The Moral Law Preserves Societal Order

The concept behind the horror franchise *The Purge* (a series I have neither seen nor would I encourage others to see) illustrates well what life would be like if the law of God did not restrain sinful men whatsoever. The basic plot for each film is that during one twelve-hour period every year, all crime is legal. No rules, no penalties, nothing. Whatever you want to do you are free to do. In all the franchise boasts five films and is set to release a sixth. It seems that moviegoers can't get enough of seeing what life would be like if there were no fear and no censure, if all hell suddenly broke loose.

---

7 From the hymn "Amazing Grace" by John Newton.

The Moral Law is God's instrument for the preservation of societal order and peace. It keeps the dystopian future envisioned by *The Purge* from becoming a full-blown reality. All men, converted or not, have a sense of the wrath of God against sin and so are curbed from embracing their sin to the fullest degree. It keeps those who are totally depraved by nature from becoming utterly depraved—as evil as they possibly could be. God produces this restraining fear through two primary channels: first, internally through the law written on the heart of man (Rom. 2:15), and second, externally through the civil magistrate as it exercises the power of the sword against wrongdoers (Rom. 13:4).

Channel 1: The Law in the Heart

Just as there are two basic types of fear in Scripture, so too are there two senses in which Scripture speaks of the law being written on the heart. One, in a redemptive sense limited to believers (Jer. 31:33), that is renewing them "in the will and affections, by inclining and delighting them to do good on solid grounds"; and the other, in a general sense common to all men where they possess a basic sense of right and wrong.[8]

When God created man, He made them "male and female, with reasonable and immortal souls, endued with knowledge, righteousness, and true holiness, after His own image; having the law of God written in their hearts…" (WCF 4:2). Despite Adam and Eve's fall into sin, the image of God in them was not utterly destroyed nor the law written on their hearts completely ebbed away. Their sense of the law was severely corrupted, but sufficiently intact to leave them and all their descendants without excuse for their rejection of God's self-revelation in nature (Rom. 1:20) and within their own hearts.

---

8 Burgess, *Vindiciae Legis,* 66.

Romans 2:14-16 describes the Moral Law's presence and consequences within the heart of unsaved men:

> For when Gentiles, who do not have the law, by nature do what the law requires, they are a law to themselves, even though they do not have the law. They show that the work of the law is written on their hearts, while their conscience also bears witness, and their conflicting thoughts accuse or even excuse them, on that day when, according to my gospel, God judges the secrets of men by Jesus Christ.

Contextually, Paul, ever the lawyer, is heading-off a possible objection to God's future judgment of Gentiles who sinned "without the law" (i.e. without knowing the Ten Commandments as revealed at Sinai). The question may have sounded something like this: "How is it right for God to judge the Gentiles according to the Moral Law if they have no knowledge of it?" It is a question of God's justice. Paul's response is, "God can justly condemn Gentiles for violating the Moral Law because they *do* know it, albeit not in its written, Mosaic form."

Paul submits the Gentile's external adherence to the Moral Law (v. 14, "For when Gentiles, who do not have the law, by nature do what the law requires...") and the internal wrestling of his conscience (v. 15, "...while their conscience also bears witness, and their conflicting thoughts accuse or even excuse them") as irrefutable proof that the Moral Law is written on his heart and that God is perfectly just in holding the sinner accountable for violating it. Whether he fully acknowledges his sin or not, deep down he knows in his heart of hearts that he is guilty before God and will have to answer for the sins he has committed. And so, lest he compound his misery at the day of Christ's coming, the unregenerate sinner fearfully stays his hand from indulging in his sin to the degree he would like.

Channel 2: The State and the Sword

The second channel of restraining fear works from the outside in, when man observes the painful, temporal consequences inflicted upon evildoers by the civil magistrate.

In Romans 13, Paul says that all governing authorities "have been instituted by God" whether they are obedient to God or not (v. 1). Good or evil, God is sovereign over the placement of them all. When they operate according to their divinely ordained purpose, earthly governors "are not a terror to good conduct, but to bad" (v. 3). The one who is in authority is "the servant of God, an avenger who carries out God's wrath on the wrongdoer" (v. 4b). Because all governing authorities have been instituted by God they are therefore obligated to "punish those who do evil and to praise those who do good" (1 Pet. 2:14). They are not free to call evil good and good evil (Isa. 5:20), rather they are to rule according to *God's* standard of justice (Ps. 82:1-4) and will answer one day for how they stewarded their positions of authority.

When the civil magistrate consistently punishes evil, it deters others from committing the same evil. Conversely, when the civil magistrate neglects its duty to punish evil or gives criminals mere slaps on the wrist for crimes that merit severer punishments, this encourages and emboldens the offender and those around him to commit those same crimes again. As soon as one affirms the "T" in TULIP (that is, total depravity), law-enforcement makes good sense. The civil magistrate, in and of itself, is not a "necessary evil" but a practical necessity to prevent human evil from consuming the world. While there is no shortage of debate among legal scholars as to the best means of deterrence (financial penalties, prison sentences, execution, etc…), Scripture is clear that God designed the civil magistrate to inspire fear, prevent lawlessness, and promote righteousness: "Would you have no fear of the one who is in authority? Then do what is good, and you will receive his approval, for he is God's servant for your good. But if you do wrong, be afraid, for he does not bear the sword in vain" (Rom. 13:3b-4a).

The Perennial Question

This raises the question of extent—to what extent is the civil magistrate responsible to punish evil? If all governing authorities are God's servants, doesn't it make sense that they should punish *all* transgressions of the Ten Commandments and not just some? What good servant only performs a portion of what his master commands? And if governing authorities are not expected to enforce all Ten Commandments, which of them should they enforce and why?

With the transition from a theocratic kingdom under the Old Testament to an exclusively spiritual kingdom in the New Testament (John 18:36) the church and state now have related, but distinct roles. Both serve God, but not in an identical manner. It is the responsibility of the church to discipline its members for sin and it is the state's responsibility to punish its citizens for crimes. There are two important steps that one must take to arrive at this conclusion:

Step 1: The Distinction Between the Spiritual and Civil Kingdoms
Calvin called the distinct responsibilities of the church and state the spiritual and temporal jurisdictions:

> ... intimating that the former species has reference to the life of the soul, while the latter relates to matters of the present life, not only to food and clothing, but to the enacting of laws which require a man to live among his fellows purely, honorably, and modestly ... we may call the one the spiritual, the other the civil kingdom.[9]

---

9 Calvin, *Institutes*, 3.19.15.

To the spiritual kingdom God has given the keys of the kingdom (Matt. 16:18), that is the power to exercise church discipline as its tool for dealing with matters relating to eternal life. To the civil kingdom God has given the power of the sword to maintain order among men in matters relating to this present life (Rom. 13:4). Though there will be instances wherein the interests of the church and state overlap (e.g. murder, theft, sexual assault, etc.), their purposes must not be confused nor conflated into one.

Because the church no longer exists as a political body as it did under the Old Covenant (WCF 19:4), not only has the obligation to keep the Civil Law passed away but so too has the church's authority to enforce judicial laws. Nowhere in the New Testament are church leaders instructed to use the judicial laws of the Old Testament for the purpose of disciplining the church's members or combating unbelief in their neighbors. Vern Poythress, in his excellent book, *The Shadow of Christ in the Law of Moses,* writes, "God wants us to eradicate false worship using His proper means, the means of prayer and evangelism."[10] The Apostle Paul is in full agreement; the church is engaged in spiritual warfare and so its weaponry is spiritual to match, "For though we walk in the flesh, we are not waging war according to the flesh. For the weapons of our warfare are not of the flesh but have divine power to destroy strongholds" (2 Cor. 10:3-4). Joshua's earthly military campaign against the peoples of the land was typological of the spiritual campaign of the greater Joshua—Jesus Christ—against sin, the flesh, and the devil. Christ waged this war during His earthly ministry and continues to wage it even now through the church militant (Eph. 6:10-20). When Jesus gave His disciples the Great Commission, the church's spiritual commission to make disciples of all nations, the means

---

10 Vern S. Poythress, *The Shadow of Christ in the Law of Moses*, 1st ed (Brentwood, Tenn: Wolgemuth & Hyatt, 1991), 310.

He appointed were not earthly but spiritual—the ministry of the Word and the administration of the sacraments (Matt. 28:19-20). The church's mission and the means of accomplishing its mission are both spiritual in nature under the New Covenant.

By the same token, because the state no longer exists as a spiritual entity as it did under the Old Covenant, it no longer possesses the authority to rule in matters that fall within the church's spiritual jurisdiction exclusively (e.g. infrequent church attendance, teenagers disrespecting their parents, lust, gossip, critical speech, etc…). Though Paul does say that the civil magistrate is God's servant for His people's good (Rom. 13:4), this does not mean that the church and state pursue the same exact good. For example, is it good to preserve our neighbor's life in accordance with the sixth commandment? Yes. Is it also good to worship God in the manner that He has prescribed in His Word? Yes. The sixth and second commandments are both moral goods, but that does not make them the same good. They are separate commandments after all. So it is with the goods pursued by the church and state; God created the church for the good purpose of nurturing the soul and the state for the good purpose of maintaining temporal peace.

Furthermore, even if one denies that the church and state are to pursue distinct but related goods, to infer from Romans 13 that they are to pursue a common good in one and the same manner (i.e. the state should punish its citizens for all the same reasons that the church disciplines its members) is not supported by the text. Consider the example of how the various members of a football team (let the reader understand) have a united goal (the end zone) but do not achieve that goal in the same way. If the quarterback does the running back's job and the tackle does the tight end's job, the team cannot achieve so much as a first down. So it is with the church and the state. When the state maintains temporal good in a manner that accords with the principles of biblical justice and operates within the bounds of its divinely delimited authority, this creates an environment wherein the church is free to pursue its higher good of proclaiming the gospel to a lost and broken world.[11]

Step 2: The Distinction Between Sins and Crimes

Assuming one grants Calvin's argument that the church and state have distinct purviews, this still requires that we define what is properly within the purview of each institution. As I have already asserted, the church is responsible for disciplining sin and the state is responsible for punishing crimes. So what is the difference between sins and crimes? The traditional answer is that all crimes are sin but not all sins are crimes.[12]

Vern Poythress helps fill out this pithy distinction between the two:

> A sin is any offense against God. A crime is a legally reprehensible offense against another human being. Sin describes damage to our relation to God; crime describes damage to fellow human beings. The two are not identical. Every crime is a sin, but not every sin is a crime. For example, coveting is a sin but not a crime. In the Old Testament no fixed civil penalty attaches to coveting. It is not a "chargeable offense" from the point of view of civil justice. Coveting (unless it

---

11 Another illustration that comes to mind is the relationship between general and special revelation (See Psalm 19 and how the world [vv. 1-6] and the Word [vv. 7-14] work in harmony with each other). They are related in so far as they both reveal the one true God, but they are used by God for two distinct purposes. General revelation reveals that there is a God and leaves men without excuse whereas special revelation reveals how to be reconciled to God through Christ.

12 Civil disobedience to civil laws that are contrary to the Moral Law is the obvious exception to this rule. See Daniel chapters 3 and 6 for Old Testament examples and the Apostles' answer to the Sanhedrin when told to stop preaching Christ: "We must obey God rather than man" (Acts 5:29).

leads to overt actions like theft or murder) does not directly damage other human beings, and so the state has no business in overseeing a process of restoration and retribution… Every crime is a sin because God commands us to love our neighbors. Hence, every offense against a neighbor violates God's commandment and represents rebellion against Him.[13]

As Poythress rightly shows, even in the Old Testament there was not a corresponding civil penalty for *every* violation of the Ten Commandments. In his commentary on Romans 13:3-4, John Murray agrees that the civil magistrate's authority has always been limited to the punishment of overt actions and not the inner attitudes of man's heart which only God can know: "It is with the *deed* that the magistrate is concerned. Paul speaks of the good and evil *work*. It is not the prerogative of the ruler to deal with all sin but only with sin registered in the action which violates the order that the magistrate is appointed to maintain and promote."[14] Only God knows the heart and so only He can (and will) administer just recompense for any and all transgressions of the Moral Law (1 Sam. 16:7; Jer. 17:10). The state cannot occupy the place of God and nor should Christians want it to.

So not all sins are crimes, but what then are crimes? Poythress continues:

But not every sin is a crime, because some offenses against God do not *directly* harm other human beings…Offenses against fellow human beings are within its [the state's] jurisdiction, but offenses against God are not (except, of course, if they are *also* offenses against human beings)…The state is not given authority to punish human actions on the basis of distant

---

13 Poythress, *The Shadow of Christ in the Law of Moses,* 294.

14 John Murray, *The Epistle to the Romans,* The New International Commentary on the New Testament (Grand Rapids, MI: Eerdmans, 1995), 151, emphasis added.

indirect effects that those actions might have…The state must restrict itself to the human acts that actually cause damage to other human beings; it is not given authority to meddle in the more inward precursor acts that feed the heart of sin. [15]

In short, for a sin to rise to the level of a crime it must have direct, horizontally damaging impacts upon our neighbor's outward estate (viz. life, property, good name, etc…). The harm done to the offended party must be concrete and measurable. The state cannot punish wrongdoing based upon the effects that a given action *may* have but on the observable effects it has had or necessarily will have (e.g. the traumatic effects of indecent exposure, which are well documented). One does not need to use their imagination to anticipate the disorder and injustice that would result if civil magistrates took it upon themselves to act on matters where the offense given is internal, subjective, and couched in therapeutic terms—it's happening already (e.g. "He didn't use my preferred pronouns and negatively affected my mental health … His deadnaming me caused me psychological harm … I was traumatized by his hateful comments").

Though sins like idolatry, false worship, and taking God's name in vain may, and often do, have negative impacts upon our fellow man, those sins are directly against God and only indirectly scandalizing to others. Because it is impossible to measure *how* negatively impactful such offenses are, (How do we measure the degree to which a person is scandalized? What do we do if one person is more scandalized by a certain action than another person? Whose conscience determines the severity of the crime?) it is, consequently, impossible to determine corresponding penalties. For the punishment to fit the crime, we need to know how heinous the crime was to

---

15 Poythress, *The Shadow of Christ in the Law of Moses*, 294, 296, 297.

begin with. So long as a person is not being *forced* to break the first, second, or third commandments like Daniel, Shadrach, Meschach, and Abednego were, then it is right to say that man is not necessarily or directly affected when his neighbor commits these sins.

There is a fine but noteworthy difference between being an offended party and being an affected party. In a physical assault case, the offended party is the one who was physically assaulted. The family of the offended party will no doubt be negatively affected by the assault; they will experience emotional turmoil and spend considerable time caring for the victimized. But, properly speaking, the family members are not the ones against whom the offense was committed.

There is another significant difference between objecting to something and actually being harmed by it. As a Presbyterian, I find the excesses of contemporary worship disorderly and contrary to the clear teaching of Scripture (1 Cor. 14:40). I wish that my brothers and sisters in Christ would not worship this way, but, strong as my distaste for false worship is, to say that such worship does me actual harm goes a step too far. It is often the case that false worship in one place begets false worship in other places, but it is not true in every case. If we are not careful to distinguish indirect and *possible* effects from the direct and necessary effects of wrongdoing then we will slide very quickly into a type of moral subjectivism that will not resolve but compound society's problems.

Christians in the World

The answer for the spiritual declension we are witnessing in the Western world is not to outsource the church's job to the state. Both have specific jobs to do and must stay in their respective lanes for each to accomplish its mission.

To be sure, part of the reason that the West is in such dire straits morally is because Christians, by and large, have muted their prophetic voice and shrunk back from declaring the will of God for and to the civil magistrate. The reason for this silence is prompted in part by hostility from those outside of the church, but there is also a more subtle internal pressure that has made many fearful of advocating for biblical morality in the public square. Mantras like, "Don't make politics your religion" or "Don't be a culture warrior" are often used to rebuke sincere believers for being outspoken on issues like abortion, the LGBTQ+ agenda, and same-sex marriage. By no means am I denying that politics can and has become an idol to many. Like anything else in life, politics has the potential to take our eyes off of the kingdom of God and to fixate them upon the kingdoms of man. Real as this danger is, the church institutionally, and Christians individually, can do no less than to call on civil rulers to perform their God-given duties and, as Calvin said, "to employ all the power that they possess, in defending the church and maintaining godliness."[16] No, the church is not a political organization, it should not endorse political candidates or tell Christians how to vote on every issue—such activities are outside of the church's spiritual jurisdiction. Even so, individual Christians as members of the spiritual and civil kingdoms have the responsibility to live obediently to Christ in both spheres and to pray for and call on all people, including "kings and all who are in high positions," to submit to the lordship of Jesus Christ (1 Tim. 2:2).

If the church institutionally and Christians individually remain silent and hide the light of God's Word as it concerns the responsibilities of the state, how can we expect the state to start ruling righteously? The church can and must maintain that

---

16   John Calvin, *John*, The Crossway Classic Commentaries (Wheaton, Ill: Crossway Books, 1994), 418.

faithful balance between its narrow mission of making disciples of all nations *and*, as the occasion calls for it, to remind earthly governors that they will answer to the King of kings and Lord of lords for how they ruled in this life: "Now therefore, O kings, be wise; be warned, O rulers of the earth. Serve the Lord with fear, and rejoice with trembling. Kiss the Son, lest he be angry, and you perish in the way, for his wrath is quickly kindled. Blessed are all who take refuge in him" (Ps. 2:10-12).

The Second Use: Grace Shown to All

The second use of the law is a gift of God to fallen humanity as a whole and especially to the bride of Christ. The world, though fallen, could be in a far sadder condition than it is. All that it would take for *The Purge* to become a reality is for God to withdraw His hand but for a moment. God would be perfectly just to put no restraints on human wickedness and allow unbelievers to suffer at the hands of evil men. Adam made man's bed, and God would have been right to let us all lie in it. But instead, God has written His law upon the hearts of all men and set up earthly governors to keep evil in check, so that even His *enemies*, those who say in their heart "There is no God" (Ps. 14:1), would enjoy a measure of happiness, peace, and safety in this life. What a demonstration of God's common grace! Though David was speaking covenantally in Psalm 103:10, his words can rightly be applied to God's treatment of all men in this life: "He does not deal with us according to our sins, nor repay us according to our iniquities." And when believers stop to remember that Christ Jesus, who is head over all things and King of His church, is restraining and conquering all of His and our enemies through the law as a constant vanguard for our sakes (WSC Q. 26), then we are further amazed at God's saving grace shown to us. The law is one of God's many instruments whereby He works all things together for His glory and our good (Rom. 8:28).

5

The Third Use

The Law as Map

"Now what?" Perhaps that's the question you're asking if you've believed on Christ already for your salvation. As you look in the rearview mirror you can see how God used the Moral Law to drive you to Christ for pardon and how He protected you from your own and your neighbor's unmitigated evil desires through a civil fear of the law. You're thankful for all that God has done through the law, but now, with the rest of your Christian life ahead of you, the usefulness of the Moral Law seems far less clear. On the one hand, you don't want to disregard the Moral Law entirely and "continue in sin that grace may abound" (Rom. 6:1); on the other hand, you don't want to slide into a subtle works righteousness where your faithful obedience to the law is seen as the means of maintaining your right standing with God (Gal. 3:3). Is there a place for the Moral Law in the life of the believer that safely navigates between the ditches of legalism on the one side and lawlessness on the other? Does the Moral Law have any use beyond convicting us of our remaining sin?

The clear testimony of Scripture is that the law, in its third use, acts as a map to guide believers in the way of holiness. When God saves us from the bondage of our sin, He does not leave us aimless; the Moral Law gives clear direction to the people of God for how to order their lives for His glory. Like the pillar of cloud and fire that guided Israel during its wilderness wanderings, the Moral Law is a lamp to the believer's feet and a light to his path, leading him all his life long until he enters the Savior's promised rest (Ps. 119:19; Prov. 6:23).

That many have never considered the law in this capacity is quite remarkable, considering Calvin believed the third use was "the principle use, and more closely connected with its proper end" than the first two uses.[1] When verses like Galatians 5:1, "For freedom Christ has set us free; stand firm therefore, and do not submit again to a yoke of slavery," are understood to mean that grace frees believers from the obligatory power of the Moral Law, we begin to see why so many Christians are reluctant to study and apply the law in their lives.[2] "Under the gospel," the reasoning goes, "there is only *can* and *should*. Any notion of *must* destroys grace and makes obedience servile and slavish." But this oversimplifies matters as there are countless *musts* in Scripture directed specifically to those who have already been redeemed. Paul's letter to the Romans was addressed to those who were "loved by God and called to be saints" (Rom. 1:7), Colossians was written for "faithful brothers" (Col. 1:2), and Peter's epistles were sent to the "elect exiles" in Asia Minor (1 Pet. 1:1) and yet none of these writers shied away from moral imperatives! Neither Peter, Paul, James, John, the writer of Hebrews (or Jesus Himself for that matter) were undermining grace when they commanded obedience to the Ten Commandments. The law can and does

---

1 Calvin, *Institutes,* 2.7.12.

2 An examination of the immediate context reveals that Paul was not even talking about the Moral Law in Galatians 5:1, but the Ceremonial Law and its various regulations.

serve the purposes of the gospel when used in the proper way. To demonstrate that this is the case, this chapter will explain why the third use of the law has historically fallen on hard times, and offer just a handful of scriptural arguments for why believers are required to follow the Moral Law as their rule of life.

Disuse of the Third Use

Behind much of the neglect of the third use of the law is a laudable desire to safeguard the purity and sufficiency of God's grace in the gospel. If justification by faith alone is, as Luther quipped, the doctrine upon which the church stands or falls, then believers should be vigilant and cry down any and all attempts to mix the blood of Christ together with the works of sinful men. But this vigilance has led some to be overly suspicious of those who reason from Scripture that believers are not merely encouraged but *required* to live in obedience to God's law. Seventeenth-century antinomians are a key historical example of those who argued that the Moral Law is stripped of its obligatory force once a believer is converted to Christ. Quoting John Saltmarsh, one of the leading antinomians of the period, Ernest Kevan writes:

> The believer is now under grace, and there is 'no Moses now.' It can do no other than bring the believer into bondage if he does things 'meerly as commanded from the power of an outward commandment or precept in the Word,' and such a relation to the law produces 'but a legal, or at best but a mixt obedience and service of something a finer hypocrisie.'[3]

In other words, Saltmarsh contended that it was wrong-headed for believers to obey the law simply because it was commanded. Doing so, he reasoned, would result in begrudging and insincere obedience. To be sure, believers have a veritable array of

---

3 Ernest F. Kevan, *The Grace of Law: A Study in Puritan Theology* (Morgan, Pa.: Soli Deo Gloria, 1999), 169.

reasons and motives for why they should adhere to the law's commands. If the *only* reason we obey the law is "because God says we have to," there is something wrong with our hearts. But to say that obeying a biblical command *because* it is commanded brings the believer into a state of spiritual bondage goes too far. The problem with Saltmarsh's view is that he has unwittingly set up a false dichotomy between duty and love—the two are not mutually exclusive. Kevan writes:

> Law does not end when a man delights to obey it: it is still there to be honoured and enjoyed in the obeying of it. A sovereign is no less a sovereign because his subjects love him. God does not cease to be God as soon as His people are reconciled to Him; He does not forfeit all rights to command as soon as people come to love Him. There is, therefore, nothing incompatible between love and obedience; for in the truly sanctified life there is loving obedience and obedient love.[4]

Samuel Rutherford illustrates the relationship between love and duty this way: "Gospel-motives vary not the nature of duties; as a Master may command the same duties to his sonne and his servant, upon different grounds...."[5] Does the son's love for his father or the father's love for his son in any way diminish the authority of the father to command or the authority of the command itself? By no means. The content and authority of the command to the servant and to the son are the same, though, in the case of the son, the motive behind the father's command differs in this—the father commands his son in paternal love and the son, in turn, submits in filial love to his father. The same is true of God's commands under the gospel— they maintain their authoritative power *and* they are issued in

---

4 Kevan, *The Moral Law,* 3.

5 Samuel Rutherford in Ernest Kevan, *The Grace of Law: A Study in Puritan Theology,* 175.

love. And because God, in the gospel, has freely justified us by His grace and made us His own through the adoption of the Spirit, our duty to love and serve Him is actually *increased*. Obeying the Moral Law is only contrary to the gospel if the goal is to accomplish through our obedience what only Christ could accomplish through His. Not all obedience is legalism.

A Place for Obedience
In recent days, the Reformed and Presbyterian world has had to grapple over the doctrine of progressive sanctification. Over the course of these debates, some have explained sanctification as simply looking back on your justification. Others have redefined sanctification to mean "getting used to your justification." What is lacking in both of these definitions is any sense that the believer, in sanctification, is "enabled more and more to die unto sin, and live unto righteousness" (WSC Q. 35). Why no mention of our Spirit-enabled ability to say no to sin and yes to obedience from the heart instead? In the Shorter Catechsim, we are told that repentance unto life involves the believer turning from his sin unto God "with full purpose of, *and endeavour after, new obedience*" (WSC Q.87, emphasis added). Where is this duty to pursue new obedience in "sanctification is merely looking back on your justification"? What these deficient definitions indicate is that there are still many who, like the seventeenth-century antinomians, equate the pursuit of obedience to God's law with legalism. Their allergy to works-righteousness has caused them to throw the baby out with the bathwater.

When sanctification is conceived of as a mere spectator of justification, like an awe-inspired fan cheering in the stands, when it loses its own distinct character apart from justification, it should come as no surprise to us that the idea of actively killing sin and pursuing obedience are dropped from sanctification's definition. Why so? Because justification is not according to works. And if sanctification is only an extended reflection upon and appreciation for our justification, then there is effectively no proper place left for faith-inspired effort or the pursuit of holiness in the Christian life. Every biblical imperative is either contrary to the gospel or reduced to a suggestion or pious advice. Make no mistake, we should be overwhelmingly grateful for and look back to our justification. Gratitude is among the chief motivations of the Christian life. But true love and gratitude will express themselves in obedience to all that God commands. Jesus told us this is so—"If you love me, you will keep my commandments" (John 14:15).

Now that we've seen that God's commanding and our obeying are not at odds with the gospel, we are ready to examine a few of the many places in Scripture where believers are told to follow God's law as a map and why they are to do so.

Obeying *For* Life vs. Obeying *From* Life

When a sinner comes to Christ in saving faith, Scripture teaches that he is a new creation, for "The old has passed away; behold, the new has come" (2 Cor. 5:17). This new identity in Christ produces an objectively new relationship to and subjective attitude toward the law of God.

There are two ways in which man is said, objectively, to be under the Moral Law. He is under the law either as a Covenant of Works or, as Paul says, "under the law of Christ" (1 Cor. 9:21; Gal. 6:2).

Prior to conversion, all mankind are born under and condemned by the Covenant of Works. The Covenant of Works that God extended to Adam as the representative head of humanity required perfect obedience to the Moral Law that was written on Adam's heart and to God's positive command not to eat of the tree of the knowledge of good and evil. Had

Adam obeyed, he would have inherited eternal life for himself and all his posterity, but because Adam failed, not only he but all mankind descending from him by ordinary generation (Jesus Christ being the one exception due to His supernatural conception by the power of the Holy Spirit in the womb of the virgin Mary) fell into an estate of sin and misery (WSC Q. 17). When Adam fell, he took us all down with him; we "sinned in him, and fell with him, in his first transgression" (WSC Q. 16). Scripture teaches that by virtue of this inherited guilt from Adam's fall, we are born "children of wrath by nature" (Eph. 2:3). This is what David meant when he confessed, "Behold, I was brought forth in iniquity, and in sin did my mother conceive me" (Ps. 51:5). Coupled with this, our own inability to perfectly obey the Moral Law renders us accursed: "Cursed be everyone who does not abide by all things written in the Book of the Law, and do them" (Gal. 3:10).

In the Covenant of Works there is no such thing as partial credit for partial obedience—there is only pass or fail. For our obedience to be acceptable to Him who is perfectly and entirely holy, our obedience to the law must be perfect and entire. As James said, "For whoever keeps the whole law but fails in one point has become guilty of all of it. For He who said, 'Do not commit adultery,' also said, 'Do not murder.' If you do not commit adultery but do murder, you have become a transgressor of the law" (James 2:10-11). In the same way that a collectible trading card, even if it is flawless in every other respect, cannot be considered mint if it suffers from just one bent corner, so neither can our obedience, even if it is 99.99 percent in conformity to God's law, satisfy the inflexible terms of the Covenant of Works. It is all or nothing and no one ever has or can offer such obedience, save Jesus Christ the righteous.

Christ, through His obedient life and substitutionary, atoning death, satisfied the terms of the Covenant of Works on behalf of His people. Believers, though freed from obedience to the law as a Covenant of Works, are still under the Moral Law but for a radically different purpose—they are subject to the law of Christ. But what *is* the law of Christ and what does it mean to be under it?

In 1 Corinthians 9:19-23, Paul defends his ministry against Jewish detractors who were accusing him of being hostile to the law of God.

> For though I am free from all, I have made myself a servant to all, that I might win more of them. To the Jews I became as a Jew, in order to win Jews. To those under the law I became as one under the law (though not being myself under the law) that I might win those under the law. To those outside the law I became as one outside the law (not being outside the law of God but under the law of Christ) that I might win those outside the law. To the weak I became weak, that I might win the weak. I have become all things to all people, that by all means I might save some. I do it all for the sake of the gospel, that I may share with them in its blessings.

Because Paul did not enjoin Gentile converts to be circumcised or to observe the various Jewish feast days and dietary laws, many Jewish believers thought that Paul was an antinomian, that he was anti-law.

Paul asserts that he is indeed no longer under the law (v. 20), but not in the way that his critics suppose. Paul did not believe that the gospel freed him from the obligation to keep the Moral Law. That is not the law in view in verse 20. Paul's point is that because Christ fulfilled the *Mosaic* Law he is under no obligation to abide by it in his ministry to the Gentiles. To those unconverted Jews still living under the terms of the Mosaic Law, Paul was free to "become as one under the law" (v. 20). He was free to observe Jewish rites and ceremonies in the interest of appealing to his kinsmen according to the flesh.[6] But to those who were "outside the law" (i.e. Gentiles), Paul was equally free to become as one who was outside the law. He was willing to become all things to all people in order that both Jews and Gentiles would believe in the gospel (v. 23). The freedom Paul has in mind is methodological freedom; not freedom from obedience to the Moral Law. Paul maintains that he is still under the Moral Law, but not for the sake of working for life, but for the sake of honoring and glorifying Christ who gave him the gift of eternal life.

The other place where Paul mentions the "law of Christ" is in Galatians 6:2. In his concluding exhortations to the church in Galatia, where the Judaizers were sowing seeds of discord between Jews and Gentiles, Paul writes, "Bear one another's burdens, and so fulfill the law of Christ." Paul's language here mirrors what he wrote earlier in Galatians 5:14.[7]

When one considers the striking parallels between these verses, it becomes abundantly clear that the "law of Christ" in

Galatians 5:14	Galatians 6:2
For the whole law [Moral] is fulfilled in one word:	and so fulfill the law of Christ
"You shall love your neighbor as yourself."	Bear one another's burdens

---

6 Paul's decision to circumcise Timothy (Acts 16:3) and his refusal to circumcise Titus (Gal. 2:3) demonstrates that there was no one-size-fits-all approach even to the evangelization of the Jews. Because the Judaizers insisted that circumcision was necessary for salvation, Paul did not have Titus circumcised lest he appear to be supportive of their false teaching. But, in the case of Timothy, to remove a possible stumbling block to the Jews that Paul and Timothy would encounter on their missionary journey, Paul had Timothy circumcised. Paul was willing to abide by the provisions of the Mosaic law for a time, but only so long as it remained clear that one did not need to keep the Law of Moses in order to be saved.

7 See also Rom. 13:8-10 and James 2:8 where the "royal law" is clearly synonymous with the law in Romans and Galatians, seeing that it is fulfilled in the same way: "You shall love your neighbor as yourself."

Galatians 6:2 is the same law in Galatians 5:14, which is the Moral Law.[8] Paul commanded his readers to fulfill (i.e. obey) the law—but in love to Jesus Christ.

In *The Marrow of Modern Divinity* the Scottish theologian, Edward Fisher (1627–55), explains how the Moral Law relates to the Covenant of Works and the law of Christ. Written as a dialogue, one character, Evangelista, is asked by another, "Then sir, I pray you, proceed to speak of the law of Christ; and first let us hear what the law of Christ is." Evangelista answers:

> The law of Christ, in regard of substance and matter, is all one with the law of works, or covenant of works. Which matter is scattered through the whole Bible, and summed up in the decalogue, or Ten Commandments, commonly called the moral law, containing such things as are agreeable to the mind and will of God, that is, piety towards God, charity towards our neighbor, and sobriety towards ourselves. And therefore was it given of God to be a true and eternal rule of righteousness, for all men, of all nations, and at all times. So that evangelical grace directs a man to no other obedience than that whereof the law of the Ten Commandments is to be the rule.[9]

Notice how Evangelista says that the substance of the Covenant of Works and the law of Christ is the same—the Moral Law. This is the first step in understanding why believers are still expected to keep the Ten Commandments even after they have

---

8 In saying that the "whole law" is fulfilled by loving our neighbor, neither Jesus, Paul, nor James are making the same mistake that adherents of the Social Gospel do when they reduce the gospel to "Love thy neighbor." Our duty as believers, first and foremost, is to love God with all our heart, soul, strength, and mind and then, in turn, to love our neighbor. When Paul mentions the "whole law," he does so in a context where the overarching concern is how believers should treat one another. So, when Paul says that loving our neighbor fulfills the whole law, he means that it fulfills the whole law with respect to our duties toward our neighbor.

9 Edward Fisher, *The Marrow of Modern Divinity*, ed. Thomas Boston, (Ross-shire, Scotland: Christian Focus Publications, 2015), 185.

been freed from the Covenant of Works—because the grace of Christ directs us to no other standard of obedience than that encapsulated in the Moral Law!

Nomista, one of the dialogue partners, grants Evangelista's definition and notes, "But yet, sir, I conceive, that though (as you say) the law of Christ in regard of substance and matter, be all one with the law of works, yet their forms do differ." And right he is! The substance (content) is the same but the purpose or reason for adhering to it changes under the gospel.

Evangelista responds:

> True, indeed; for (as you have heard) the law of works speaks on this wise, 'Do this and thou shalt live; and if thou do it not, then thou shalt die the death' but the law of Christ speaketh on this wise, 'And when I passed by thee, and saw thee polluted in thine own blood, I said unto thee, when thou wast in thy blood, live' (Ezek. 16:6). 'And whosoevereth liveth and believeth in me, shall never die' (John 11:26). 'Be ye therefore followers of God, as dear children: and walk in love as Christ hath loved us' (Eph. 5:1-2)…Thus, you see, that both laws agree in saying, 'Do this.' *But here is the difference; the one saith, 'Do this and live'; and the other saith, 'Live, and do this'; the one saith, do this for life; the other saith, Do this from life.*[10]

What a beautiful description of the difference between justification according to the law and according to the gospel! In the Covenant of Works our personal obedience to the law is the necessary *precondition* of eternal life ("Do this and live"). But under the gospel, our personal obedience is the necessary and inevitable *consequence* of having been made alive by God's grace ("Live and do this"). As Samuel Bolton says, "We preach obedience to the law, but not as the Papists do. They preach obedience as a means to justification; we preach justification

---

10 ibid., 185-86. Emphasis added.

as a means to obedience. We cry down works in opposition to grace in justification, and we cry up obedience as fruits of grace in sanctification."[11] We are only able to "do this" once we have been made alive by the regenerating work of the Spirit. Obedience then cannot precede justification, but it does inevitably follow it in sanctification.

This same "live, and do this" order is reflected in the giving of the Ten Commandments themselves. Before God spoke the ten imperatives of the Decalogue, Moses records that God spoke all these words: "I am the LORD your God, who brought you out of the land of Egypt, out of the house of slavery" (Exod. 20:2). God starts with the indicative, what He sovereignly did for Israel's salvation, before moving on to what Israel must do as His redeemed people. Not since Adam broke the Covenant of Works has the law been revealed for the purpose of working *for* life. God has always revealed it as a tool to be used in our sanctification to teach us what living *from* life looks like practically.[12]

John Colquhoun echoes Fisher when he writes, "Eternal life is, by the perfect obedience of their adorable Surety, already merited for them; and therefore, though they are under every obligation to obey from life, they are under no obligation to obey for life."[13] There is a world of difference between those two prepositions, obeying *from* life and obeying *for* life, and oh what a difference it makes in the heart and mind of believers when they see their obedience to the Moral Law in this new and positive light!

---

11 Samuel Bolton, *The True Bounds of Christian Freedom*, 69.

12 ibid., "Walk in the duties of the law, but with a Gospel spirit. The law is to be acknowledged as a rule of sanctification, but it is to be rejected in respect of justification" (220).

13 John Colquhoun, *The Law and the Gospel*, 184.

Believers Keep the Law Because God Is Their Creator

Even before God voluntarily condescended and made the Covenant of Works with Adam in the Garden, the Westminster Confession affirms that by virtue of having been created "reasonable creatures," humans "do owe obedience unto Him as their Creator…" (WCF 7:1). God's giving us life is, by itself, a sufficient reason for believers to obey His commands. As that great psalm of thanksgiving, Psalm 100:3, says, "Know that the LORD, he is God! It is he who made us, and we are his; we are his people, and the sheep of his pasture." David supplies two rationales for his readers to give thanks to God— because He made them and redeemed them to be His people. John Colquhoun acknowledges that grace, when it releases the sinner from the bondage of the law as a Covenant of Works, does not and cannot release man from the law of nature: "Seeing they do not cease to be creatures by becoming new creatures, they are, and ever will be, obliged to yield personal obedience to the moral law as a rule of life, and that by the sovereign authority of the Father, the Son, and the Holy Spirit, their Creator."[14] So long as the Creator/creature distinction remains intact (and it always will), so too will the creature's obligation to yield obedience to his Creator. We were made by God and so we are to live *for* God in all we do.

Believers Keep the Law Because They Were Redeemed to Keep It

How would you respond to the question, "What were you saved *for*?" I suspect that many of us would answer, "To spend eternity with God in heaven," which is absolutely correct. The great goal of Christ's work is for us to be with Him where He is (John 14:3; 17:24). But there is a great deal of time between now and then, so what are we to do in the meantime? What is God's purpose for us *now*?

---

14 John Colquhoun, *The Law and the Gospel,* 119-120.

In Paul's letters to the Thessalonians, we find a church that had become confused concerning the end times. In 1 Thessalonians 4:13-18, Paul assures the church that those who have died already will not be excluded from the general resurrection at Christ's second coming as many feared. Then in 1 Thessalonians 5:1-11, Paul tells the Thessalonians to always be vigilant, to resist complacency and sloth, because they were fully aware "that the day of the Lord will come like a thief in the night" (v. 2). In their attempt to plumb the depths of God's secret will (i.e. on the exact timing of the second coming) they had neglected His revealed will for their lives. Paul calls them away from speculating on matters that only God can know (Deut. 29:29), and to focus on what they can and must know for certain, "For you know what instructions we gave you through the Lord Jesus. For this is the will of God, your sanctification…" (1 Thess. 4:2-3a). God does not expect us to know where His providence will lead us tomorrow, but He does hold us accountable to know and to do what is our duty today. Paul wrote something similar to Titus saying that Jesus "gave himself for us to redeem us from all lawlessness and to purify for himself a people for His own possession who are zealous for good works" (Titus 2:14). The answer to "What would God have me do today?" is always, "Be zealous for good works." That, we know for certain.

To personalize matters even further, Paul says in Romans 8:29 that God predestined us "to be conformed to the image of His Son…" We were saved to look like Christ. And wherein is the image of Christ more clearly reflected than in the Ten Commandments? If we really want to grow to be more like Jesus, we will find ourselves using the law more and more as the roadmap for our sanctification. As Samuel Bolton said so succinctly, "The law sends us to the gospel for our justification; the gospel sends us to the law to frame our way of life."[15] In Ephesians 2:10 Paul writes, "For we are his workmanship, created in Christ Jesus *for good works*, which God prepared beforehand, that we should walk in them." We were redeemed for a purpose. We were created at first to obey and recreated in Jesus Christ to obey unto His glory.

Believers Keep the Law Because They Are Commanded to Love
All moral duties that God reveals in His Word are reducible to the two great commandments, love for God and love for neighbor. The aim of every individual commandment of the Decalogue is the same—love. John Lennon's famous line actually works quite nicely here as a summary of the Moral Law, "Love is all you need."

In Romans 13:8-10, Paul tells his readers that love is the fulfillment of the law:

> Owe no one anything, except to love each other, for the one who loves another has fulfilled the law. For the commandments, "You shall not commit adultery, You shall not murder, You shall not steal, You shall not covet," and any other commandment, are summed up in this word: "You shall love your neighbor as yourself." Love does no wrong to a neighbor; therefore love is the fulfilling of the law.

In saying that love fulfills the law, Paul is by no means suggesting that our love fulfills the law to the same qualitative degree as Christ's love or that our love achieves the same goal. Only Christ's love (demonstrated through His obedience to the Moral Law) was sinlessly perfect and perfectly satisfied the law's demands for salvation. Christ's fulfillment was vicarious and redemptive (He fulfilled the law for our sakes) whereas our fulfillment of the law is eschatological, meaning, whenever we love we are simply realizing God's grand purpose for our lives.

---

15 Samuel Bolton, *The True Bounds of Christian Freedom*, 72.

Just as a hammer fulfills the purpose for which it was created when it drives a nail, so too do we fulfill the purpose of our creation when we love God and our neighbor as ourselves.

Adam and Eve enjoyed perfect love in the Garden. They loved God and one another with a pure and selfless love, and yet their love was tentative. It was subject to change, and it did change when they turned their love inwardly upon themselves and fell into sin. And even after our conversion, on this side of heaven, believers' love will never be pure or entire—but we need not be discouraged. One day, when Jesus returns in glory, the redeemed of the Lord will enjoy perfect love once again, only this time it will be permanent. We will be made "perfectly blessed in the full enjoying of God to all eternity" and participate in the overflowing, overbrimming love of our triune God together as one (WSC Q.38).

Believers Keep the Law Because Their Hearts Delight in the Law

When a dead sinner is raised to newness of life in Christ, Paul says, "There is therefore now no condemnation for those who are in Christ Jesus. For the law of the Spirit of life has set you free in Christ Jesus from the law of sin and death" (Rom. 8:1-2). The freedom of which Paul speaks encompasses our exemption from God's condemnation through Christ's condemnation in our place (Rom. 8:3) and the ability to live in obedience to the law in a way that truly pleases the Lord. This was impossible according to our former nature, "For the mind that is set on the flesh is hostile to God, for it does not submit to God's law; indeed, it cannot" (Rom. 8:7). The good news of the gospel is not only that the blood of Christ pardons us of all our sin, but that by the Spirit's power we are given new hearts that willingly submit to God's commands (Ezek. 11:19, 20; Jer. 31:33).[16]

---

16 Samuel Bolton, "Before [justification], we obeyed, but out of compulsion of conscience; now we obey out of the promptings of nature, which, so far as it works, works to God, as naturally as stones move downward or sparks fly

In his treatise, *Glorious Freedom*, Richard Sibbes beautifully describes how the believer's new spiritual condition inspires a radically new disposition toward the law of God:

> We are now by the Spirit at liberty to delight in the law, to make the law our counsellor, to make the Word of God our counsellor. That which terrified and frightened us before is now our direction. A severe schoolmaster to a very young pupil becomes later, as the pupil grows, a wise tutor to guide and direct. So, the law that terrifies and whips us when we are in bondage, till we are in Christ—it scares us to Christ—that law afterward comes to be a tutor, to tell us what we shall do, to counsel us and say this is the best way. And we come to delight in those truths when they are revealed to us inwardly. And the more we know, the more we want to know, because we want to please God better every day. [17]

When Sibbes speaks of liberty he uses it to describe something deeper than the ability to *do* the right thing (which is remarkable in its own right), he speaks at the level of the believer's desires—"We are now by the Spirit at liberty to delight in the law." This is significant. In life it is possible to have the ability to do something, but unless that ability is accompanied by a desire to do it, whatever that thing is will remain undone. In salvation, God gives the believer the ability *and* the desire to obey the law. In Philippians 2:12-13 Paul says, "…work out your own salvation with fear and trembling, for it is God who works in you, both to will and to work for his good pleasure." That God gives us the desire ("to will") and the ability ("to work") to obey should be a source of profound encouragement to the Christian. Our desire for obedience tends to wax and wane. We are not yet unchangeably holy as we will be when

---

upward. Thus, then, it is that we preach the law, not in opposition to, but in subordination to the gospel…" (*The True Bounds of Christian Freedom*, 75).

17 Richard Sibbes, *Glorious Freedom: The Excellency of the Gospel Above the Law*, Puritan Paperbacks (Edinburgh: Banner of Truth Trust, 2000), 41.

Christ returns. We still feel the nag and pull of remaining sin and experience the temptations and provocations of the devil every single day. But however faintly burning our desire may feel at times, God will never allow it to be snuffed out entirely. Even when we are backslidden our hearts are never completely satisfied in our sin. The heart of the believer, at some level, yearns for a renewal of fellowship with his God. Like the prodigal son who finally came to his senses and returned to his father's house, so too will every sincere believer, no matter how far or for how long he has wandered, desire and return to his God in faith and repentance.

There is the saying that people often use when asked whether they enjoy what they do for a living; they'll say, "I've never worked a day in my life." The believer can say something similar with regard to his obedience to the Moral Law. Is obeying the law hard work at times? Absolutely. Scripture speaks of straining forward toward what lies ahead (Phil. 3:13), striving to enter through the narrow door (Luke 13:24), and enduring sorrows while suffering unjustly (1 Pet. 2:19). But, because we love the one for whom we work, we consider all the toil not worth comparing to the glory that awaits us and the joy that God grants us when we live in conformity to His commands (Rom. 8:18).

Believers Keep the Law Because They Need Constant Guidance
Psalm 119, the longest psalm in the Psalter, is King David's extended meditation on the beauty of God's Word. In verse 9 David asks, "How can a young man keep his way pure? By guarding it according to your word." David understands himself well enough to know that sin and temptation are always close at hand and that hiding God's Word in his heart is absolutely essential to keep him from sinning (Ps. 119:11). And while this may appear to be beneath the dignity of mature believers, Calvin cautions, "Let none of us deem ourselves exempt from

this necessity, for none have as yet attained to such a degree of wisdom, as that they may not, by daily instruction of the Law, advance to a purer knowledge of the divine will."[18] We need our Savior every hour, and we need His law to lead us deeper and deeper into the knowledge of His will. All of us like sheep have gone astray and will go astray unless we keep in step with our Good Shepherd who uses His Law to direct and correct us. The lyrics to the hymn, "Come, Thou Fount of Every Blessing," describe the state of all our hearts when not tethered to the Word of God and to His law: "Prone to wander, Lord, I feel it, prone to leave the God I love." The answer for this wandering is to lay God's Word up in our hearts and to practice it in our lives (WSC Q. 90). And as we follow God's law as a map; we should feel profoundly comforted knowing that He will never lead us astray. We can trust Him with all of our hearts and rest assured that He will make our paths straight, leading us into deeper and deeper communion with Him, wherein true joy is found (Prov. 3:5-7).

Believers Keep the Law Because It Glorifies God
The mark of a good gardener is a fruitful garden. Whenever I turn on an episode of *Gardner's World* with Monty Don, the gardener of gardeners, I am always amazed by his green thumb. The hedges, fruit trees, the flower blooms in his garden are all exquisite. They are a testimony to his skill and prowess as a gardener. When believers bear fruit in keeping with their repentance (Luke 3:8), when the fruit of the Spirit abounds in their lives, God is glorified in them (Gal. 5:22-23). We are to bear the fruit of righteousness to the "glory and praise of God" (Phil. 1:11). We obey because we desire that God should receive the glory and honor due to His name.

---

18 Calvin, *Institutes,* 2.7.12.

Jesus told His disciples that they were the light of the world and that their light ought to shine before men. This shining is nothing other than the performance of good works in conformity to God's law. If the world's darkness is its evil deeds (John 3:19), then the light that Jesus says is fundamental to our identity as Christians is good deeds done in faith and love for our Savior. And what does Jesus say is the purpose of our obedient shining? "So that they [those belonging to the world] may see your good works and give glory to your Father who is in heaven" (Matt. 5:14-16, cf. 1 Pet. 2:12). We obey the law for the sake of God's glory and for the sake of our witness to the unbelieving world. Transformed lives are a strong argument for the life-changing power of the gospel. One preacher has said before that our lives are a living sermon which none can refute. So how is your preaching? Is your manner of living such that the power of the gospel in you is not only believable, but irrefutable? We must walk in a manner worthy of our calling; in a way that adorns the gospel we profess.

I can think of no better way to conclude our study of the law but by quoting the first question of the Shorter Catechism—"Man's chief end is to glorify God and to enjoy Him forever." This is *why* we live, and move, and have our being. The gospel beckons us to come and die; to die to the reign of sin and living for ourselves and to live instead for Him who for our sake died and was raised (2 Cor. 5:15). So start living for God today. Go and use His law as your rule of life and know that when you do so, your heavenly Father delights in your obedience.

Conclusion

The Moral Law is good. That much, I hope, has been made clear throughout this study. The Ten Commandments are nothing less than ten profound blessings from the finger of God. When the law is used in the way that God designs, it is, by the blessing of the Spirit, an instrument for good in the lives of believers. It offers conviction, protection, and direction. Like the rest of God's Word, the Ten Commandments are a lamp to our feet and a light to our path (Ps. 119:105). We cannot be justified by our obedience to the law but nor can we be truly sanctified apart from its guiding influence. The law charts the course for our sanctification—it is the mold to which we conform. To grow in Christ-likeness is to grow both in our appreciation for and obedience to the law of God. It is impossible to be like Jesus without being conformed to the law that He came to fulfill.

I also hope that this study has deepened your love not only for the law but for the gospel also. Loving one should naturally lead us to love and value the other. Because when we study carefully the nature and the purpose of the law, it necessarily brings us to a fuller understanding of all that Christ has accomplished for us in the gospel. When the law reveals the vileness of our sin and the hopelessness of our situation, we see the beauty of Christ and His righteousness and the extent of His love in condescending to pay the penalty for our sins. When the law maintains a degree of civil order in the world through law-inspired fear, we see God's long-suffering and patience with the world generally (John 3:16-17), and His covenantal love for His people particularly. God keeps human evil in check through the law in order to preserve His church to the end of the age according to His promise. The law is God's protective rod with which He beats back the ravenous wolves that seek to devour His chosen sheep. And as the law directs our hearts and our steps toward heaven, we are all the more in awe of our Savior who upheld the law in perfect submission to His Father's will, even as He died upon the cross for our sins. In this we have a picture of what ought to characterize our obedience, a willingness to offer the whole of our lives as a pleasing sacrifice to our God who alone is worthy of all our worship and all of our service (Rom. 12:1).

So if you haven't already, consider this my humble appeal to you, the reader, to take the law from behind the museum glass, dust it off, and start putting it to good use. And like me, I expect, you'll look back in time and be forever grateful that you did.

Appendix 1

On Pedagogical Images of Christ

Many, while granting that it is forbidden to *worship* using images of the Father, Son, or Holy Spirit in corporate worship, still maintain that it is permissible to use images of the incarnate Christ for pedagogical (teaching) purposes. The argument for pedagogical images typically goes like this: "Since Christ was truly God *and* truly man we are free to depict His humanity as we would that of any other human being. So long as we qualify that we are only depicting Christ's human nature and not His divine nature, we are not violating the prohibition against making images of Christ *as God.*"

There are three key problems with this position. First, such an argument divides the two natures of Christ that are inseparably united together in His one person forever (WCF 8:2). Thomas Watson argues, "It is Christ's Godhead, united to His manhood, that makes Him to be Christ; therefore to picture His manhood, when we cannot picture His Godhead, is a sin, because we make Him to be but half of Christ—we separate what God has joined, we leave out that which is the chief thing which makes Him to be Christ."[1] Christ, in the incarnation, never existed only as a man. He was, is, and continues to be God and man in two distinct natures and one person forever (see the Chalcedonian Creed). Because an image cannot adequately capture the full glory of Christ according to either nature, every image is necessarily a false image and also a violation of the third commandment.

Second, the hard division between instruction and worship is, to my mind, far too neat and impossible to maintain. The goal of all Christian instruction, whether corporate, familial, or private, is worship. All of life, it has been said, is worship (Rom. 12:1).[2] Such being the case, to limit the scope of the second commandment to say that images of Christ are prohibited *only* in corporate worship but permissible in every other context is tantamount to saying that family worship and personal Bible study are not at all worshipful. But they are! Whenever I am teaching members of my congregation or my own family about the person and work of Christ, my desire is for them to worship Him with a greater love and devotion right then and there. Christian instruction that doesn't aim to be worshipful isn't worthy of the name "Christian." Because believers are *meant* to worship in their hearts and minds whenever they think of Christ, any unsanctioned representation of Him necessarily becomes to the beholder what the golden calf was to Israel—a cheap imitation of Him whose beauty and glory is far beyond our imagining.

The third problem with pedagogical pictures of Christ is that they are unnecessary. God's Word says of itself that

---

1 Thomas Watson, *The Ten Commandments* (Edinburgh: The Banner of Truth, 2009) 62.

2 Even as I say this, I in no way want to blur the clear distinctions between the spheres of corporate, family, and private worship. Each is a legitimate form of worship, but that does not mean that the same rules that apply in one sphere necessarily apply in the others (e.g. the sacraments are to be administered in the corporate sphere only [1 Cor. 11:17]).

it is sufficient to thoroughly equip men and women, boys and girls, for every good work to which He has called them (2 Tim. 3:16). Everything necessary for life and godliness, for doctrine and devotion, is clearly articulated in the pages of Scripture, including what must be believed concerning the person and work of Christ. Westminster 1:7 says this of Scripture's sufficiency:

> All things in Scripture are not alike plain in themselves, nor alike clear unto all: yet those things which are necessary to be known, believed, and observed for salvation, are so clearly propounded, and opened in some place of Scripture or other, that not only the learned, but the unlearned, in a due use of ordinary means, may attain a sufficient understanding of them.

That being said, if it is necessary for one to confess Jesus Christ as the Son of God and the Son of Man (i.e. the hypostatic union) for salvation, then we must conclude that Scripture already communicates this truth in some place and in such a way that both the learned and unlearned, the old and the young, can sufficiently understand it.

Many well-meaning Christian parents who use images of Christ to teach their children will say, "We need pictures of Jesus in order to teach our children about the incarnation. Our kids are visual learners. They find them helpful and we don't want to hinder their spiritual growth by taking them away." Again, by no means am I calling into question the motives or sincerity of such parents. As a pastor, I rejoice whenever I see Christian parents taking seriously their responsibility to train up their children in the way they should go (Prov. 22:6). Nevertheless, the fact that the Bible doesn't come with inspired pictures of Jesus—or even much by way of physical description—should tell us something.[3] The absence of images indicates that they are in no way necessary for children to understand the reality of the incarnation. The Word alone is able to teach our children all that they need to know—the gospel is the power of God to salvation (Rom. 1:16). Faith comes by *hearing* and hearing by the Word of God (Rom. 10:17). We are a people who live by faith and not by sight.

There is nothing that a picture can teach us that the Bible doesn't teach already, and that infallibly so. The Word of God is like a child's toy that comes with the batteries already included—it requires no external inputs from us in order to function properly. God's Word together with the blessing of the Spirit is able to convict, convert, and instruct without the help of man-made images. There is a saying that we often use in our visually inclined culture: "A picture is worth a thousand words." In the case of images of our Lord, the second commandment tells us, "The Word is worth more than a thousand pictures."

---

3 Presbyterians weren't isolated in this view as the contiental Reformed tradition likewise opposed images of Christ. See Heidelberg Catechism question 98, which asks: "But may not images be tolerated in the churches, as books to the laity?" The answer given: "No: for we must not pretend to be wiser than God, who will have his people taught, not by dumb [silent] images, but by the lively preaching of his word."

Appendix 2

A (Brief) Argument in Favor of Sabbath Laws

As noted in chapter two, the traditional breakdown of the Ten Commandments is that the first table (commandments 1-4) outlines our vertical duties (directly to God) and the second table (commandments 5-10) outlines our horizontal duties (directly to our neighbor). This distinction, though helpful, should not be seen as absolute.

The fourth commandment, I would argue, has a foot in both tables of the Decalogue in that direct, vertical *and* horizontal effects often result when we fail to honor the Sabbath day as we should. Of course, the priority of the commandment is first and foremost on the vertical: "Remember the Sabbath day, to keep it holy. Six days you shall labor, and do all your work, but the seventh day is a Sabbath to the LORD your God" (Exod. 20:8-10a). In Revelation 1:10, John calls the Sabbath the "Lord's Day" because the whole day is to be spent in the "public and private exercises of God's worship" (WSC Q. 60). It is His day and was appointed to be a "holy Sabbath to Himself" (WSC Q. 58). If the day belongs to the Lord, if it is all about Him, then it stands to reason that He is the one whom we ultimately offend when we fail to rest and worship as commanded. The vertical dimension is primary.

The latter half of the commandment, however, intimates that there are direct, negative, and measurable effects upon our neighbors' wellbeing when we cause them to work for reasons that fall short of necessity or mercy: "On it you shall not do any work, you, or your son, or your daughter, your male servant, or your female servant, or your livestock, or the sojourner within your gates" (Exod. 20:10). In Exodus 23:12, where the fourth commandment is reiterated, Moses makes explicit the rationale for why we shouldn't cause our neighbors to work on the Sabbath—it is so that they may rest: "Six days you shall do your work, but on the seventh day you shall rest; *that* your ox and your donkey *may have rest*, and the son of your servant woman, and the alien, *may be refreshed*" (emphasis added). Resting from our ordinary employment and recreation is not only for our own sakes but also for our neighbors'. When we cause our neighbors to work unnecessarily on our behalf, we are depriving them of the physical and spiritual refreshment they are due and in so doing are sinning against them *directly*.[1] Their restlessness is a direct consequence of our decision to "rest" in ways that God has said are not lawful on the Sabbath. It matters not whether our neighbor is willing to work on the Sabbath. Most are. But because we do not apply that same logic to the rest of the second table (for example, imagine trying to apply this same logic to murder and theft) we shouldn't apply it to the fourth commandment either.

---

1 One could also say that we "rob" our neighbor of their divinely given rest and so are guilty, at the same time, of breaking the eighth commandment against stealing. This is what the Westminster Divines mean in LC 99:3: "That one and the same thing, in divers respects, is required or forbidden in several commandments."

To be clear, I am not suggesting that the state should involve itself in *every* violation of the fourth commandment any more than it should involve itself in every violation of the sixth commandment (e.g. anger) or the seventh commandment (e.g. lust). According to Larger Catechism 119, carelessly performing the duties required of the day (i.e. worshipping half-heartedly), idleness, and needless works, words, and thoughts about our worldly employments and recreations are all violations of the fourth commandment. Yet because they do not have a direct, negative effect upon our neighbor's wellbeing they are not within the civil kingdom's jurisdiction. If implemented, Sabbath laws would need to be limited only to that which is outward, measurable, and negatively affects others, namely laboring in matters that cannot be categorized as either necessary for the preservation of life or merciful to others.

There are lots of opinions about what Sabbath laws might look like. For my part, I am not advocating for a return to American Blue Laws which, for a number of reasons, seemed to fall into the same problem of the Pharisees by creating tedious lists of dos and don'ts that often contradicted themselves.[2] The principle, however, remains: the state has been vested with the responsibility and prerogative to curb external acts that have a direct, negative impact upon the outward estate of its citizens—and this is necessarily the case whenever men and women are made to work on the day when they should be free to rest and worship their Creator.

---

2 What if instead of penalizing businesses for remaining open on the Lord's Day, the government offered tax incentives to those businesses that closed their doors?

Study Questions

Chapter 1

1. Why are the Ceremonial and Civil Laws no longer binding upon believers? Of what are they typological?

2. What does the Westminster Confession mean when it speaks of "general equity"? How does this idea help us make ethical decisions today?

3. Explain the difference between positive laws and natural law. Why is it important to maintain this distinction?

Chapter 2

1. Read and discuss Larger Catechism 99:1-8. Which of the eight rules do you think is most underutilized in interpreting the Ten Commandments today? Why so?

2. Which of the Ten Commandments do you think is least understood? Which portion of this chapter did you find most clarifying or helpful?

3. How does seeing the implicit "put on" for every "put off" in the Ten Commandments change the way we view the law? How would you respond to someone who believed that the law requires no more than it explicitly states?

Chapter 3

1. Aside from the three examples provided in the chapter, can you think of any other ways that man tries to excuse his sin? How does Scripture respond to those excuses?

2. In what sense are we freed from the Moral Law?

3. Why did God reveal the Moral Law to Moses at Mt. Sinai if not for the sake of meriting eternal life?

4. What does it mean that Christ is the "end of the law"?

Chapter 4

1. What does Paul mean when he says that the law is "not laid down for the just"?

2. In what way is fear appropriate in the Christian life?

3. If governing authorities are God's servants for our good (Rom. 13:4) and tasked with punishing evil (1 Pet. 2:14) then why shouldn't we expect them to punish violations of the first and second tables of the law?

4. What is the difference between sins and crimes? How does this difference relate to the spiritual and temporal jurisdictions?

Chapter 5

1. What explains the aversion of some to the third use of the law?

2. How does the gospel transform our relationship to the Moral Law?

3. What is the "law of Christ"?

4. How does love fulfill the law?

Also available from Christian Focus Publications ...

ENTOR

PHILIP S. ROSS

FROM THE FINGER OF GOD

The Biblical and Theological Basis
for the Threefold Division of the Law

...something for the Bible lover on every page... A real and rewarding mind-opener.
Alec Motyer, Well known Bible expositor and commentary writer

978-1-84550-601-8

From the Finger of God

The Biblical and Theological Basis for the Threefold Division of the Law

Philip S. Ross

This book investigates the biblical and theological basis for the classical division of biblical law into moral, civil, and ceremonial. It highlights some of the implications of this division for the doctrines of sin and atonement, concluding that theologians were right to see it as rooted in Scripture and the Ten Commandments as ever-binding.

Like me, you may never have thought that the division of the Law into the categories of civil, ceremonial and moral needed prolonged enquiry. When you read this book you will be glad that Dr. Ross thought otherwise. The book would be worthwhile if only for the discussion of the Decalogue or of the fulfilment of the Old Testament in the New , but there is something for the Bible lover on every page, as well as a demanding but readable opening up of a huge area of biblical enquiry, that takes us with profit from Genesis through to the Lord Jesus and his apostles. A real and rewarding mind-opener

ALEC MOTYER (1924–2016)
Well known Bible expositor and commentary writer

Christian Focus Publications

Our mission statement
Staying Faithful

In dependence upon God we seek to impact the world through literature faithful to His infallible Word, the Bible. Our aim is to ensure that the Lord Jesus Christ is presented as the only hope to obtain forgiveness of sin, live a useful life and look forward to heaven with Him.

Our Books are published in four imprints:

⟨◯⟩ CHRISTIAN FOCUS

Popular works including biographies, commentaries, basic doctrine and Christian living.

⟨◯⟩ MENTOR

Books written at a level suitable for Bible College and seminary students, pastors, and other serious readers. The imprint includes commentaries, doctrinal studies, examination of current issues and church history.

⟨◯⟩ CHRISTIAN HERITAGE

Books representing some of the best material from the rich heritage of the church.

⟨◯⟩ CF4KIDS

Children's books for quality Bible teaching and for all age groups: Sunday school curriculum, puzzle and activity books; personal and family devotional titles, biographies and inspirational stories – because you are never too young to know Jesus!

Christian Focus Publications Ltd,
Geanies House, Fearn, Ross-shire,
IV20 1TW, Scotland, United Kingdom.
www.christianfocus.com